QUALITY FOLKS

Practical Meditations

WILLIAM FORNEY HOVIS

Published by Left of Brain Books

Copyright © 2021 Left of Brain Books

ISBN 978-1-396-32174-0

First Edition

All rights reserved. No part of this publication may be reproduced, distributed, or transmitted in any form or by any means, including photocopying, recording, or other electronic or mechanical methods, without the prior written permission of the publisher, except in the case of brief quotations embodied in critical reviews and certain other noncommercial uses permitted by copyright law. Left of Brain Books is a division of Left of Brain Onboarding Pty Ltd.

Table of Contents

Preface	1
Quality Folks	2
Weight and Measure	4
Servants on Horses and Princes on Foot	6
The Banner Class	8
The Beauty of Holiness	10
A Sweet-Smelling Savor	13
Untempered Mortar	16
The Simple Life	19
Unnumbered	22
Heat and Brilliancy	25
The Withered Hand	28
Pious in Spots	31
Sunlight and Moonlight	33
Color Blind	35
Making Faces	37
Weak Spots	39
Clean Dirt	41
The House by the Side of the Road	44
The Back Yard	47
Strayed Sheep	49
Theory and Practice	51
Holding Fast	53
Sour Grapes	56
Paying Back	58
Life Filled Full	61
The Fraternity of Sorrow	63

I Won't Do It	66
Letting the Truth Slip	68
A Tree Planted by the Rivers of Waters	70
Good Conversation	73
The Day's Work	76
The Heart's Inclination	78
Puffed Up and Built Up	81
Angels' Food	83
Crooked Ways	85
The Signs of an Apostle	87
Self-Mastery	90
The School of Experience	93
A Blemished Offering	96
The Price of a Worthy Work	99
Made Over	102
Projected Efficiency	104
The Diet of the Soul	107
The Medicines of the Soul	110
A Large Place	112
A Divided Heart	115
The Man of God	117
Work and Worship	119
Remembering One's Faults	122
Immortality	125
The Heart of Christmas	129
Gains and Losses	131

PREFACE

I HAVE given these pages to the press in the hope that they might have a blessed ministry. Some of the sentiments are original, and some have been suggested by the written thought of others. No attempt has been made to be doctrinal, nor even theological, except in a very practical sense. With no desire to disparage the value of the mystical in worship, I have sought to emphasize the fact that one's religion is his life and that the quality of one's deeds is the determinant of his essential value.

The themes have not been selected with any idea of logical sequence, nor with any particular thought of inter-relation except that the prevailing purpose has been to quicken interest in the qualities of life which must be elemental in the divinest types of human character. The quotations at the beginning of each meditation have been selected with care from a wide field of literature, both as to time and character, and are designed to be suggestive of collateral reading. The number of chapters is not arbitrary, but, being fifty-two, naturally suggests a subject for consideration for every week in the year.

The object of the volume is to furnish a little solid religious food so concentrated as to contain much strength in small compass. Each study may be read in a few minutes. On account of the brevity of the composition the style is necessarily terse and epigrammatic. I shall be satisfied if the succeeding sentences are so provocative of thought as to cause the reader to write out in terms of his own experience the sermons of which these scattering phrases are only the bony framework.

W. F. H.

SOUTH BEND, INDIANA, 1908.

QUALITY FOLKS

"They shall be Mine, saith the Lord of hosts, in that day when I make up My jewels."—*Malachi iii, 17.*

"Wealth is a weak anchor, and glory can not support a man; this is the law of God, that virtue only is firm, and can not be shaken by a tempest."—*Pythagoras.*

"Let not the wise man glory in his wisdom, neither let the mighty man glory in his might, let not the rich man glory in his riches; but let him that glorieth glory in this, that he understandeth and knoweth Me, that I am the Lord which exerciseth lovingkindness, judgment, and righteousness in the earth: for in these things I delight, saith the Lord."—*Jeremiah ix, 23, 24.*

"Wood burns because it has the proper stuff in it; and a man becomes famous because he has the proper stuff in him."—*Goethe.*

"QUALITY FOLKS" are not necessarily those whose affluence would class them with "the four hundred," nor yet those whose wisdom and superior endowments have enabled them to contribute something substantial to the world of knowledge and history. With no wish to disparage the power of gold in the hand of Goodness, and with no desire to detract by the merest trifle from the worth of learning, let us rather emphasize the thought that God's quality folks, whether rich or poor, wise or untutored, high or low, are those who love His law and who think upon His name.

The world has a wrong way of estimating values. It calls the proud happy. It is deluded by bulk and glitter. It is awed by exalted position. It lays too much stress upon quantity and not enough on quality; even the elements by which it determines quality are more usually accidental than intrinsic. Its judgment is poor because it deals too much with transitory things which are seen, and forgets that the things not seen are eternal. It fails to remember that the quality of life is determined by what it is, and not by what it has. It does not seem to understand that, while wealth and wisdom may be of great advantage to those who possess them, in the long run they can not measure fortunes with faithfulness.

God is exceedingly opulent; the heavenly Father has riches untold. He has an option on all the diamond mines in the universe, and He is busy gathering a remarkable collection of jewels. He is selecting His gems with great care; He can not be deceived on value. Sometimes He finds a precious stone in the rough which has to be polished before its full value is apparent. His treasures are human hearts. Good folks are God's folks, the kind He finally gathers to Himself and calls "jewels." Real "quality folks" have hearts that are gems.

The quality folks with whom God associates must be rich, but their treasure must be in heaven; they must be wise, but their wisdom must be unto salvation. God's best people are workers. They have endowments and are bidden to occupy until the Master comes, and are cautioned not to misuse their talents in an attempt to use them. Where one's treasure is there his heart will be, and to have a place in God's jewel-box means a soul-life with the virtues of a precious stone.

If we knew as much about people as God does, we might change our minds about who are the quality folks of our town. We are liable to misjudge a man because he is rich or wise, or both. We put wrong estimates upon men's piety because we do not see nor hear them make their prayers. We are liable to associate worship with words and outward attitude. The story is told of a little girl, left to, take care of an invalid mother, who worked until her hands were out of shape with toil. One day, after their mother had gone, she was talking to her little sister about heaven and how the Savior surely expected His children to pray. She began to cry, for fear that because she had not had time to pray much she would not be permitted to enter. The younger child, with the insight of innocence, said, "Show Jesus your hands, and maybe He will let you in." What a fine interpretation of the heart of Love! The little tot was right; her sister wore the badge of service, and her twisted hands were the marks of her apostleship. She was rich toward God. She had the quality of a jewel. It is concerning such souls that the good God says, "They shall be Mine in that day when I gather together My gems." Yes, to belong to God's quality folks one must be rich, but it is a wealth that the poorest may have. Heirs to the kingdom must achieve their possession through service. The determining quality of heaven's aristocracy is goodness.

WEIGHT AND MEASURE

"The Lord is a God of knowledge, and by Him actions are weighed."
—*1 Samuel ii, 3.*

"And I lifted up my eyes, and saw, and, behold, a man with a measuring line in his hand."—*Zechariah ii, 1.*

"How little do they see what is, who frame their hasty judgments upon that which seems."—*Southey.*

"If we do not weigh and consider to what end life is given us, and thereupon order and dispose it arightly, pretend what we will as to arithmetic, we do not, and can not number our days in the narrowest and most limited signification."—*Clarenden.*

"The Lord seeth not as man seeth; for man looketh on the outward appearance, but the Lord looketh upon the heart."—*1 Samuel xvi, 7.*

IN the prophecy of Isaiah the Lord declares that His ways are not man's ways, neither His thoughts man's thoughts; but as the heavens are higher than the earth, so are His thoughts and ways higher than man's. When the venerable Samuel was sent to look over the sons of Jesse and to select a king to reign in the place of Saul, he was struck by the natural nobleness and majesty of the appearance of Eliab and cried out, "Surely the Lord's anointed is before me;" but the Lord said: "No, you are mistaken; the Lord seeth not as man seeth, for man looketh on the outward appearance, but God looketh on the heart."

The study suggests a contrast between the ways of God and those of man. Man uses a yard-stick, and God a balance; man makes a quantitative, God a qualitative analysis. The one errs through lack of knowledge, the other knows the heart and weighs the actions. Man feels it necessary "to keep up appearances," sometimes even at the expense of honor; God "desireth truth in the inward parts" regardless of how the outside looks. The one measures greatness, the other weighs goodness.

One of man's most glaring weaknesses is that he is unduly attracted by show. He reduces everything to figures. He deems one rich if he have so many dollars, so many acres of land, so many houses, so many reins of power; one is mighty by certain calculable spaces. He often makes the mistake of thinking that one's life consisteth in "the abundance of the things which he possesseth;" he is liable to be dazed by the spectacular and deceived by tinsel. He drops the diamond because it is small, and snatches up the limestone because he can get it in big chunks. The man with a measuring line estimates greatness by extent, capacity, volume. To him a great city is one of vast spaces; a great wall is one of massive proportions. The man with a balance must ever consider internal excellence. He is concerned not so much with the shape, and form, and size of the object as with its character, temper, worth.

Man is interested in external dimensions largely because he is unable to see or know the inside. Opulence, wisdom, and exalted position count with him. Wherever he is seen with his line he is calculating the superficial area, and if he should ever be found with a pair of scales he will be weighing by avoirdupois. His judgments, based on appearances, are often in error, because knowledge of the outside is hardly half-knowledge. It is only when he breaks through the surface into the inner mysteries that he thinks God's thoughts over after Him. When man comes out of some secret place of communion with the Almighty and announces that he has seen something, he is called a discoverer, a prophet, or an inventor.

God is interested in the intrinsic value of things. He asks not how great, but how good? His interest in the inside does not lessen His concern about the outside, but He puts first things first. He knows that it is only when the "King's daughter is all-glorious within" that her clothing is of wrought-gold," and that he who seeks the kingdom of God first, will find other things added in due form and season. He has full knowledge of all things and His judgments are, therefore, right.

Man's real life is his heart-life. Before you can know him you must go back into the secret center of his being. Some people have the best side and some the worst side out. Before the worth of a life can be justly determined it must be known not only as it seems, but as it is. Quality of life is more important than quantity. God weighs actions. The vital question must ever be, Is thy heart right? Deeds are not measured as to number, extent, or size; they are weighed. To fall below the standard is to be found wanting. To be full weight is to be fit to enter heaven.

SERVANTS ON HORSES AND PRINCES ON FOOT

"I have seen servants on horses, and princes walking as servants upon the earth."—*Ecclesiastes x, 7*.

"From the lowest place, when virtuous things proceed, the place is dignified by the doer's deed."—*Shakespeare*.

"A fine coat is but a livery when the person who wears it discovers no higher sense than that of a footman."—*Addison*.

"Foolish men mistake transitory semblances for eternal facts, and go astray more and more."—*Carlyle*.

"Beware so long as you live of judging men by their outward appearances."—*LaFontaine*.

THE text is a striking picture of a very common truth. The author suggests that, though in the one instance the person posed as a prince, there was such an apparent incongruity between himself and his position, to his own disparagement, that it seemed evident that he was lifted above his real worth. In the second case there was still a disagreement, but the value of the man was unbefogged by his position. There is a sense in which the station makes the man, but more often the person makes the place. The mere fact that a servant rides a horse does not make him fit to be a prince, and the mishap that makes a monarch go on foot does not change his nature. A real prince is princely whether fortune permits him to ride or misfortune forces him to walk.

Position is not always a criterion of worth. Policy and what is commonly known as "a pull" too often govern the selection of a man for a given place. Even with those in high authority favoritism is liable to count. The phenomenon of "servants on horses" is often seen in politics. It is necessary to know more about a man than that he is the president of a life insurance company, a postmaster, or a senator, before one is justified in calling him a prince.

What one is in character, motive, spirit, he is in reality, whether he live in a king's palace or a peasant's hut. Circumstances may affect the appearance, but they do not necessarily change the quality. What happened to Job, the rich emir of the Bible drama, when he was smitten with such staggering loss, was only a change in his mode of life, and not a change of heart. Sitting upon an ash-pile bereft of family, robbed of flocks, loathsome with disease, and scorned by friends, he is still a prince. To melt gold is to change its form, but not its worth.

It is more honorable to be a worthy man on foot than a fool on horseback. Cato, the elder, on being asked why he had no statue erected in his honor, replied that he would rather men should ask why he did not have a statue than why he had. If one have real worth, somebody will find it out whether he publish the fact or not. He who fills a low place well will be invited higher. It is better to be too large for a small place than too small for a large one. The mounted servant is in danger of being asked to surrender his seat, while the princely footman is sure to be promoted.

Judge no man by appearances, for they sometimes lie. Transitory semblances do not always represent eternal facts. He who seeks for high position without regard to merit is a servant who wants to be a rider and to appear to be a prince. He has not learned the genius of greatness expressed in the Master's word, "Whosoever would be chief among you, let him be a servant." It is always safe to take the lowest seat. A princely footman will always be asked to ride. A prince on foot is princely none the less; a servant on horseback is only a servant still.

THE BANNER CLASS

"Thou hast given a banner to them that fear Thee."—*The Psalms lx, 4.*

"Talent and worth are the only eternal grounds of distinction. To these the Almighty has affixed His everlasting patent of nobility, and these are they which make the bright, immortal names to which our children, as well as others, may aspire."—*Miss Sedqwick.*

"Them that honor Me I will honor."—*1 Samuel ii, 30.*

"Rest satisfied with doing well, and leave others to talk of you as they please."—*Pythagoras.*

"Because he hath set his love upon Me, therefore will I deliver him; I will set him on high, because he hath known My name. He shall call upon Me and I will answer him; I will be with him in trouble; I will deliver him and honor him."—*The Word of God.*

MARKS of distinction are not lightly esteemed by anybody. Every ambitious student strives for the honors of his class. There is no delight quite equal to that of being the chosen one, whether the selection be made on the basis of real merit or mere popularity. This is true whether the recipient of favor be a child in a kindergarten-game chosen most often by her little companions, or a man elected by his fellows to a position of distinguished leadership. I never see a lot of children playing but that I pity the tots who wait so anxiously, but are never chosen once during the game, for the disappointment ar1s1ng out of being a candidate for honors and failing to receive them is so keen.

I knew a spelling-class once in a little red schoolhouse, where the members vied with one another for headmarks. All tried, but the contest finally narrowed down to three. Why did two boys and one girl study these lessons until they could see them in their dreams? Not particularly because of the value of the prize, but because each coveted the distinction of winning, and being the hero of the class. I would n't give much for a fellow who did n't try to be an honor-man. It is right for any one to strive for the mastery if he strive lawfully.

The world's banner class affords an interesting and a somewhat amusing study. Its standards are variable and are based upon scholarship, wealth, physical beauty, art, prowess, etc. Its distinctions are sometimes dignified and sometimes ludicrous. Its affection is always fickle. The value of its banner depends upon the quality it marks. One may only be noted for being a freak. People will pay admission to see the largest man or the smallest, or a mummy, or Siamese twins. The world will talk about a man whether he be noted or notorious.

With reference to man's being, his relation to God is of primary importance. The Bible is full of statements to this effect. Too many people put everything and seek everything before God. This is unfair. If God were given His rightful place there would be no incongruity between the honors He bestows and those bestowed by men. As it is, man looks on the outside and God on the inside; man asks, Have you got any money? God asks, How did you get it? When the inside and the outside agree, the kingdoms of earth and heaven meet.

Man's distinction before his Maker depends upon the virtue of his motives, and the honor he receives depends upon the worship he ascribes to Him. Man is honored of God when he is in right relations to the world about him, and when God marks a man the stamp is seen. Shallow-hearted and small-brained people advertise themselves, but the man to whom God gives a banner has a goodness which speaks for itself. Has God given you a banner? If so, both you and others have found it out. There is honor for all who are honor-men.

THE BEAUTY OF HOLINESS

"Worship the Lord in the beauty of holiness."—*1 Chronicles xvi, 29.*

"Holiness is the symmetry of the soul."—*Philip Henry.*

"The essence of true holiness consists in conformity to the nature and will of God."—*Lucas.*

"It must be a prospect pleasing to God to see His creatures forever drawing nearer to Him by greater degrees of resemblance."—*Addison.*

"The serene, silent beauty of a holy life is the most powerful influence in the world, next to the might of the Spirit of God."—*Pascal.*

THE moment an object is invested with beauty it becomes a thing to be desired. Beauty is attractive and never lacks votaries who worship at its shrine. There is something in a man that always responds to the bewitching spell of comeliness. He may err in his judgment as to what constitutes gracefulness, but he never fails to yield to its charm. Prove that a thing is beautiful, and you create a demand for it. Even external adornment wields an influence over the shallow-hearted and unwise. Recognizing this fact, far-seeing concocters of curative cosmetics, taking advantage of a sometimes noticed feminine desire, have flooded the market with pastes and powders and lotions and liniments warranted to bleach and tint, or to fill up hollows and smooth out wrinkles, and rejuvenate blanched and faded countenances, as if beauty were a thing to be smeared on the outside! Beauty that is not deep-seated will rub off and fade.

If holiness could be seen to be the thing of beauty which indeed it is, men would seek it as a hidden treasure. The difficulty is that its visage has been marred by garblers, many of whom unintentionally misrepresent the truth. The sin against the beauty of saintliness is the sin of ignorance—ignorance of the principles and essence of righteousness. True holiness is always beautiful. It has inspired a perennial interest in the human heart in spite of the imperfections of its exhibiters. If no one has ever seen any of the beauty of holiness in you, the fault is with you, and not with holiness.

Holiness is not anything that can be assumed or merely professed. It is a quality of the heart. It is constitutional. Beauty is its inevitable aspect—the mark that God sets on virtuous living. "Pretty is that pretty does." The author of one of the proverbs says that "a fair woman without discretion is like a jewel of gold in a swine's snout." Some people are like certain flowers which are admired for their color but despised for their odor.

> "What is beauty? Not the show
> Of shapely limbs and features.
> > These are but flowers
> > Which have their dated hours
> To breathe their momentary sweets, then go.
> > 'T is the stainless soul within
> > That outshines the fairest skin."

The story is told of a gentleman who had two children—one, a daughter, very plain and unattractive; the other, a son, very fair and handsome. One day they both saw their faces in the mirror. The lad was charmed with his countenance, and commented on his beauty. The girl, sad at the sight of her plain features, and hurt by her brother's rudeness, took the matter to their father, who heard the tale and then addressed them thus: "I would have you both look into the glass every day; you, my son, that you remember never to dishonor the beauty of your face by the deformity of your actions; and you, my daughter, that you may take care to hide the defect of beauty in your person by the superior luster of your virtuous and amiable conduct." It is better to acquire beauty than to be born with it. The one must increase, the other decrease. The young man looks at his bride and sees a physical beauty and vigor of youth; the old man looks at his wife and sees a lovelier beauty, that has been refined by sorrow and perfected through suffering.

The beauty of holiness is the beauty of wholeness. It involves the whole man—physical, mental, moral. But a man may be sound and complete with reference to any stage in his development and yet be a long way from maturity. The fairness of a symmetrical soul is not the work of one day. Little by little life's harmony is written in the face. The fountain head of beauty is the heart, and every generous thought adds luster to the outward shapes of life. The inward grace of holiness has an outward, inviting charm. When holiness is really present, beauty, its complement, is always there. The average person thinks of holiness as religiousness, sanctimoniousness, piousness, which are liable only to indicate the lack of holiness. Be not deceived; holiness is simply wholeness, and wholeness is always fair.

A SWEET-SMELLING SAVOR

"An offering and a sacrifice to God for a sweet-smelling savor."
—*Ephesians v, 2.*

"Live for something. Do good, and leave behind you a monument of virtue that the storms of time can never destroy. Write your name in kindness, love, and mercy on the hearts of thousands you come in contact with year by year, and you will never be forgotten."
—*Chalmers.*

"Having every one of them harps and golden vials full of odors, which are the prayers of saints."—*Revelation v, 8.*

"Let us have faith that right makes might, and in that faith let us to the end dare to do our duty as we understand it."—*Lincoln.*

"Get thee behind Me, Satan; thou art an offence unto Me; for thou savorest not the things that be of God, but those that be of men."
—*St. Matthew xvi, 23.*

RECENTLY, while visiting the Congressional Library at Washington, as I stood in the vestibule among the marble columns and walked under the polished arches, reading the beautiful sentiments inscribed above the doors and windows and in the niches of the walls, my eyes fell upon these words:

> "Only the actions of the just
> Smell sweet and blossom in the dust,"

and immediately my mind turned to contemplate the value of a fragrant life, redolent with sweet odors and scented with the perfume of virtuous deeds. Since then I have been unable to shake myself loose from the thought that all life that is really worth while must be odorous with a "sweet-smelling savor."

The text, chosen because it contains a phrase which may be used as a center around which we may group our thoughts, is one of Paul's great sentences. Some people never speak without saying something rich; others speak much and say little. The apostle has been talking about brotherly kindness and has just said, "Be ye kind one to another, tender-hearted, forgiving one another, even as God for Christ's sake hath forgiven you," and now he says, "Imitate God" and "Walk in love as Christ hath loved us." He puts the Father's love and the Son's sacrifice on an equality. He would have us understand that Christ's sacrifice was not an offering to appease an angry God and to reconcile Him to His rebellious family, but only an act of devoted, sacrificial love, whose incense was a sweet-smelling savor to God. So from every good life there may arise in times of sacrifice the fragrance delightsome to God and man.

Savor is the quality that affects the taste or smell—the flavor or scent of a thing. It is applied to taste or odor, or to both combined. Salt has a certain taste or savor, without which it is worthless. A rose has likewise a scent or savor. Isaac asked his son to make him a savory meat, which meant that it should be both pleasant to taste and smell. According to the ancient idea, God's part in the burnt-offering or sacrifice was the sweet-smelling odor. Difference in savor is an essential difference. Paul said, "One star differeth from another star in glory," and so one might say, "One peach differeth from another peach in flavor; one flower from another flower in perfume; one man from another man in savor."

A person is repulsive or attractive in proportion as the savor of his actions is foul or fragrant. There is a difference between a rank weed and a carnation, expressed largely in the matter of odor. With reference to others, our likes and dislikes are based upon the flavor and odor of their lives. Hearts, like fruit and flowers, are sour or bitter or sweet, or fragrant or foul. With reference to the individual, one has the privilege and responsibility of saying himself what his own savor shall be, for God has placed at his disposal powers that can change his heart, either for better or worse.

The life that is scented with the perfume of goodness leaves sweet fragrance in its wake. Some people have a refreshing savor in their looks and words, which lingers even in their absence as the odor of a sweet smell. It was said of Evangeline that "when she passed it seemed like the ceasing of exquisite music," and the Maker of Proverbs declares, "The memory of the just is blessed, but the name of the wicked shall rot." The elements of enduring stability are always associated with the finer sentiments of the heart.

A soul diffuses its rarest fragrance when most fully imbued with the spirit of right. There is a difference between perfume applied externally and that which is breathed out of the soul within. They may smell equally sweet, but they are not equally expressive of the inner life. Religion is not something that can be put on. If it be real it must be as essentially a part of one's nature as the flavor is a part of the fruit or the fragrance a part of the flower. "A sweet-smelling savor" is the perfume of a heart that distils fragrance and simply lets it out because it can't contain it. The odor of goodness is lasting. Be good.

UNTEMPERED MORTAR

"Say unto them which daub it with untempered mortar that it shall fall."—*Ezekiel xiii, 11.*

"O, what a goodly outside falsehood hath; a goodly apple rotten at the core."—*Shakespeare.*

"Half the work that is done in the world is to make things appear what they are not."—*E. R. Beadle.*

"Were we to take as much pains to be what we ought to be, as we do to disguise what we are, we might appear like ourselves without being at the trouble of any disguise at all."—*Rochefoucauld.*

"Daubing over a bad wall with bad mortar only pre-vents its blemishes and weaknesses from being discovered, but has no tendency to strengthen it."—*Clarke.*

"The hypocrite shows the excellence of virtue by the necessity he thinks himself under in seeming to be virtuous."—*Johnson.*

IN the time of Ezekiel bricks were made of beaten earth rammed into molds, or boxes, and then dried in the sun. Such a block of dried clay would molder even if exposed to moisture, and would entirely melt away when drenched by a dashing rain. It was, therefore, necessary to daub or plaster the walls built of this material with a fine, tempered mortar of lime and sand to protect them against the weather. A wall built of sun-dried bricks and simply smeared with whitewash would stand in times of drouth, but a rain-storm would change it into a mass of rubbish. The walls of many ancient cities were made of this unbaked clay, and consequently have been washed away by the beating tempests of the centuries. Not even a vestige of the ancient ramparts of Babylon can be found.

The prophet here presents a scathing denunciation against the practice of telling lies. He likens the word of false prophets and prophetesses to a dirt-wall plastered with untempered mortar which crumbles beneath the pelting rain and is rent by the stormy wind. He represents God as being furious with anger at their untruthful pretensions; he predicts the utter demolition of the deceptive wall and the complete destruction of those who daubed it with the untempered coat. God is against the liar and the lie, and will not tolerate falsehood either spoken or acted.

The thoughtful student can not consider this portion of Scripture together with what pre cedes and what follows it, without having his mind directed to the perplexing and complicated phenomena which may be classed under the general name "prophecy." In every ancient nation there have been persons who sought to influence public opinion and action by foretelling things to be. Israel was no exception and had all the grades, from the lowest to the highest. There were those who attempted to forecast the future by magic or sorcery and the occult arts, which they believed influenced the supernatural powers which govern human destiny. Croesus sent messengers to the oracles of Delphi, Dodona, and Jupiter Ammon, to find out what would be the result of his proposed invasion of the dominion of Cyrus, and Saul, sorely pressed by the Philistines, goes to the witch of Endor, who calls up Samuel. There was also the supposed revelation of deity in dreams or "visions" or half-articulate words uttered in a state of frenzy; and finally there was the prophet in the highest sense, who, "while subject to extraordinary mental experiences, yet had a clear and conscious grasp of moral principle and possessed an incommunicable certainty that what he spake was not his own word, but that of Jehovah." But even the greatest of these were not so signally marked by the Almighty as His witnesses as to render their authority always unquestionable. It was hard then, as now, to distinguish in every instance between the voice of God and the speculations of men. Both Jeremiah and Ezekiel recognize divisions in the ranks of the prophets themselves, and discuss the difference between the true and the false.

Falsifiers did not all perish with the school of the prophets. Still is the figure of the text applicable to human experience; still are men working in clay and daubing it with untempered mortar. The practical value of this study will depend upon how the individual applies its truth to his own every-day life. You can build a wall out of pretty poor stuff and it will stand, if only it be protected by well-tempered cement. When man's poor clay is encased in God's strong armor, the bulwark seems as hard as adamant. When man tries to build a wall out of his own material without God's help, it always falls down.

A wall built of sun-dried clay and simply whitewashed may look like rock, but it can never stand the rigor of the storm. So much silk is only "near-silk;" so much character only imitation. The real value of a thing is not in appearance, but in essence. God is against all falsehood, false balances, false measures, false tongues, and every counterfeit of the genuine and cheap imitation of the real must go down in a common and unmitigated condemnation. It is impossible to deceive Omniscience. If you are obliged to work with sunbaked clay, do n't daub it with untempered mortar or your wall will crumble into dust. God's cement can make a dirt wall strong as iron. His mortar is made of prayer and every virtue of a righteous life. Put ye on the whole armor, that ye may be able to stand.

THE SIMPLE LIFE

"Not by might, nor by power, but by My Spirit, saith the Lord of Hosts."—*Zechariah iv, 6.*

"At the same time came the disciples unto Jesus, saying, Who is the greatest in the kingdom of heaven? And Jesus called a little child unto Him, and set him in the midst of them."—*St. Matthew xviii, 1, 2.*

"Nothing is more simple than greatness; indeed, to be simple is to be great."—*Emerson.*

"In character, in manners, in style, in all things, the supreme excellence is simplicity."—*Longfellow.*

"The greatest truths are the simplest: and so are the greatest men."
—*Hare.*

AFTER all, there is not so much difference between a man and a man. Men have more in common than they think they have. Life stripped of externalities is everywhere largely the same. We adorn and elaborate, and grade and classify, and fence in and hedge about, and partition and barricade, but the life back of the artificiality in every instance may be sketched in a few simple sentences. Behind the mask of equipage and trappings of culture and station and social prestige is a life at best simply characterized by birth, childhood, youth, maturity, age, and death, interspersed with the common experiences of joy and sorrow. The fences builded around individuals and classes are fancied, and not real. The music of the heart is not an epic, but a psalm. All life is keyed to love, and pain, and pity.

There are two sides to life—the outside and the inside; the person we have schooled ourselves to be, and the one we really are. The simple life is the real life; the life that rings true; the life that is free from affectation; the life God gave—unwarped, uncolored, unostentatious. It is not known by its livery; it is charitable. It is true to its own mission; it looks upon wealth and poverty, form and figure, as mere circumstances which should in no wise affect the heart. It looks upon life as grander than any or all of its accidents. It is sincere.

The simple life is an artless life. Artifice is acquired. Men have to study to deceive; they have to learn to lie. The child's life is simple, and therefore great, because it is frank, open, ingenuous, and knows no distinctions of art or station. Artificiality is destructive of simplicity. The natural flower with morning dew upon its face reveals God; the artificial, fair imitation of the real, only proves the skill of man. The moment life is taken out of its natural setting, its beauty is impaired. Mr. Emerson says it in his charming lines:

> "I thought the sparrow's note from heaven,
>   Singing at dawn on the alder bough;
> I brought him home, in his nest at even;
>   He sings the song, but it pleases not now,
> For I did not bring home the river and sky;—
> He sang to my ear,—they sang to my eye.
>
> The delicate shells lay on the shore;
> The bubbles of the latest wave
> Fresh pearls to their enamel gave,
> And the bellowing of the savage sea
> Greeted their safe escape to me.
> I wiped away the weeds and foam,
> I fetched my sea-born treasures home;
> But the poor, unsightly, noisome things
> Had left their beauty on the shore,
> With the sun and the sand and the wild uproar."

The mother rejoices in the simple beauty of her child. She never sees her offspring grimed with evil, nor bent with sin, nor even scarred with age. "In the old nest the brood is ever young. A man's best life is the child-life over which his mother crooned, before he ran away from home to feed on husks and spoil the sweetness of his soul. True grandeur is simplicity. Christ's word to hardened sinners was, "Except ye be converted and become as little children, ye can not enter heaven." Back then, to the days of the innocent heart, the unstained mind, the unpolluted lips; the days when thy heart was clean!

Simplicity is a state of mind. The rich may have it as well as the poor. It is a wholesome, good, sincere heart. The simple life is the life that God gave man, unhampered, unhindered, unalloyed. It is simply a good heart being natural. God's law is simplicity; man's, roundaboutness. O, man, wouldst thou be great, thou must be good! Simplicity is greatness.

UNNUMBERED

"Thou shalt not number the tribe of Levi. The Levites shall keep the charge of the tabernacle of testimony."—*Numbers i, 49, 53.*

"The Levites did not build the houses nor fight the battles nor plant the vineyards; but they watched over the safety of that for whose sake all houses were built, all battles fought, all vineyards planted—the inner shrine of the sanctuary—the consecration of the hearth and home. The loss of ten thousand of her soldiers would have been nothing to the putting out of her altar fires."—*Matheson.*"

"Think of a heart, a home, a business, a city, without a sanctuary in the midst! The altar is life's main ornament and its principal force—a center without which there can be no life."—*Joseph Parker.*

"A good man does good merely by living."—*Bulwer.*

THE fourth book of the Bible is called Numbers because it contains an account of the numbering and marshaling of the Israelites in their journey from the land of bondage to the land of promise. On the first day of the second month of the second year after their departure from Egypt, the tabernacle having been erected and it and the priests consecrated, Moses is commanded to take a census of the people.

There is a singular significance in the fact that he was directed to *number* the people. Each man is marked and recorded—he is number so-and-so. The emphasis is not more on the sum than the integer. God is not satisfied with mere totality. He must have an account from each number. He never loses sight of the individual; He knows if one coin out of ten is lost or if one out of a hundred of His sheep be gone astray. Herein is the emphasis of personality that every man bears an individual stamp.

But how about the Levites? They are not numbered with the rest. Have they been neglected and overlooked; uncounted or discounted because they are deemed unfit for survival? O, no; they have not been shunted from the race of life; they have been separated for special duty; they have really been given the greatest work of all. Their names were not written on the roll of warriors, but if to be unnumbered after the manner of men is to be of no account, the world is carrying a heavy freight of nuisances. The majority of lives are without a public record. Only a few are marked as leaders or their lieutenants. What, then, of the unnumbered masses, the lives without name or fame! Could they drop out of life's activities and their absence not be noticed? Nay, let no man think that he could die and a place would not be empty. In the sight of God no soul is little and no task is small.

The most telling work is always done behind the scenes. A great musician plays a brilliant concerto and a throng goes wild with cheers; but that which seems the flash of genius is only the radiance from the furnace fires of secret toil. The spectacular could not be possible without the obscure. Gorgeous flowers and tinted blossoms are only the outward manifestation of the toil of roots which work in dirt and darkness. One may pluck the bloom and hurt the root but little; but only let him pluck the root, and he has robbed the flower of life. There is a comic picture, not wholly lacking pathos, of a modern college student arrayed in flashy clothes. In the distance stands a brown-tanned son of labor, hard-handed, toil-worn, and clad in boots and jeans. The gaudy dude is dazzling, but the old-fashioned father is in fact "the man behind." The world is inclined to give the seeming undue credit and to overlook the real.

Greater than to be among the numbered is to help to build the lives that count. God bestows His crowns on people not because they are "enrolled," but because they have "served." No honest work, howe'er obscure, is mean, nor fails at length. A flower may be "born to blush unseen," but it does not "waste its fragrance on the desert air." Social settlement work is based on the belief that it is worth while for a fragrant life to drive the miasma from the desert air. Many a woman whose name is never heard beyond her humble cot has trained a child that counts. Men are made fit to be numbered in the old homestead, where influences make ineffaceable impressions. Many a man could agree with J. L. Shroy in these touching lines:

> "How oft in my dreams I go back to the day
>   When I stood at our old wooden gate
> And started to school in full battle array
>   Well-armed with a primer and slate.

And as the latch fell I thought myself free,
    And gloried, I fear, on the sly,
Till I heard a kind voice call out after me,
    'Be a good boy, good-bye.'

"'Be a good boy, good-bye,' It seems
    They have followed me all these years;
They have given a form to my youthful dreams
    And scattered my foolish fears.
They have stayed my feet on many a brink,
    Unseen by a blinded eye;
For just in time I would pause and think;
    'Be a good boy, good-bye.'"

The greatest bulwark of a nation is not its constabulary, but the humble guardians of its altar-fires. The strength of a republic lies in its intelligent and well-ordered homes. The man who founds a bad home is an enemy to the State. Burns has set the truth in fairest form:

"Then homeward all take off their sev'ral way;
    The youngling cottagers retire to rest;
The parent-pair their secret homage pay,
    And proffer up to heaven the warm request,
That He who stills the raven's clam'rous nest,
Would in the way His wisdom sees the best,
For them and for their little ones provide;
But chiefly in their hearts with grace preside."

"From scenes like these old Scotia's grandeur springs." The home is the dearest place outside of heaven, but a home without a tabernacle of testimony is only a lodging-house. Lives unnumbered by the world, but faithful to the trust of keeping the ark of the covenant, will not go uncounted by the Lord.

HEAT AND BRILLIANCY

"He was a burning and a shining light."—*St. John v, 35*.

"There are many persons the brilliancy of whose minds depends upon their heart. When they open that, it is hardly possible for it not to throw out some fire."—*Desmalis*.

"Culture of intellect without religion in the heart, is only civilized barbarism, and disguised animalism."—*Bunsen*.

"A man of intellect is lost unless he unites with it energy of character. When we have the lantern of Diogenes we must have his staff."
—*Chamfort*.

"Character is higher than intellect. A great soul will be strong to live as well as to think."—*Emerson*.

"Let your light so shine before men."—*St. Matthew v, 16*.

LET me try to paint a picture. From north to south a crooked river winds in and out through swampy glades and tracts of swaying reeds, past steep ascents and clambering terraces clothed with stately sycamores and shady oaks, and studded o'er with flowering shrubs and pale green willows, with here and there a clump of graceful palms. The valley, verdant where well watered, but barren when rising above the reach of spring-time flood, is narrow and bends to suit the river. Above the gorge some sixty feet a broad plain of blistering sand and barren waste stretches both east and west to bare and rugged hills, forming on the western border a strong contrast to the green paradise immediately girding the city of palms and roses. Here in the wilderness, apart from the rush and confusion of city life, beside the flowing stream, where the narrow limits of the yearly flood draw sharp lines between tropical luxuriance and desert barrenness, shut in on both sides by wild and stony hills, a strange man, spare of form, with fiery eye and flowing hair, rough-clad in haircloth, and leathern-girdled, lifted up his voice as the messenger of God's anointed to prepare His way. He was a man with a message. The truth he proclaimed arrested the attention and commanded the homage of all classes. He was a lofty and fearless soul, who forgot self in his fidelity to his high commission. He preached repentance as the only escape from the impending wrath of God. His voice broke the prophetic silence of five hundred years. Courageous preacher! Would anybody think of likening him to the swaying calumus stalks in the swamps by the river bank? Would any one expect to find out there amid the rigor of the wilderness a pampered son of royalty? Was he a prophet? Yes, a pre-eminent prophet—"He was a burning and a shining *lamp.*" He was not *the* light, but he came to bear witness of it.

A prophet from the Jewish point of view was not so much a seer as a fearless preacher. He was thought of as one from whom the truth shone forth as the light streams from the sun. The Hebrew word for prophet is derived from a root which means to "boil up," or "boil forth"—hence, a prophet was one who uttered by resistless impulse the rebukes and commands of the Almighty.

His words were brilliant with illuminative glory and heated with the intensity of fiery zeal. Seven hundred years before the time of John the Baptist, Amos said, "When the Lord speaks, who can but prophesy?" and later the great apostle to the Gentiles declared, "Woe is me if I preach not the gospel." A message that does not boil up out of the heart may be brilliant, but it will always lack heat.

Brilliancy without heat may be very splendid, but it has little power to rouse to life and action. Vegetation would soon lose its health and vigor and would pine away and die if it got no other light than moonlight. It is only when the sun boils forth its "deluge of summer" that

> "Every clod feels a stir of might,
>   An instinct within that reaches and towers,
>   And, groping blindly above for light,
>   Climbs to a soul in grass and flowers."

Mere intellectuality is cold and stoical. It can philosophize, theorize, analyze, dogmatize, criticise, and dream, and its cool-blooded essays can edify and enlighten: but the light which is radiant heart-heat has power in it. Slavery was put down when the hearts of the people waxed hot against it. Erasmus was a scholar, Luther was a passionate-hearted enthusiast. The former talked about the Reformation, the latter set it on foot.

With reference to character, if a choice must be made between heat and brilliancy, choose heat. It is possible for heat to reach a point where it becomes light. Ninety per cent of genius is intensity. Service is sweet when the heart is in it. The heart of the good man is the sanctuary of God in the world. The test of ability to enter the kingdom of God is a test of the heart. Christ's question on the eve of His departure was, "Lovest thou Me!" The world is in greater need of love than wisdom.

The highest type of man is one with a warm heart and a brilliant mind. A great soul is strong to live and also to think. When the heart is wrong the head is right in vain. Intellect without religion is only civilized barbarism but, on the other hand, zeal without knowledge is the frenzy of a fool. What the world needs is a fine balance of head and heart, the burning passion of unquenchable purpose, and an inerrant wisdom to give it shape.

> "Let knowledge grow from more to more.
> But more of reverance in us dwell;
> That mind and soul according well,
> May make one music as before,
> But vaster."

THE WITHERED HAND

"There was a man there, and his right hand was withered... And Jesus said, Stretch forth thy hand... And he did so: and his hand was restored."—*St. Luke vi, 6, 10.*

"Lift up the hands that hang down, and the palsied knees, lest that which is lame be turned out of the way, but let it rather be healed."
—*Hebrews xii, 12, 13.*

"Men cry, 'Put out the lame from the company of runners; they spoil the picture!' God says, 'Gather them in still more!' In His temple the lame man stands beside the gate of beauty; it mars the prospect to the eye, but it opens up a prospect to the heart."—*Matheson.*

"A great multitude of impotent folk, of blind, halt, withered, waiting for the moving of the water."—*St. John v, 3.*

THE hand is man's most conspicuous mark of differentiation from the beast. It is the most important organ of his body. It is the willing vassal of his mind. Deaf, dumb, and blind, his hand becomes his trumpet, his mouthpiece, and his eyes. Helen Keller and Laura Bridgman are striking examples of how the hand may be the intermediary between the soul and the world outside. When through age or illness his hands refuse to heed his head, it is a mark of man's decay.

The hand has much to do with art and music. One may mix his colors "with brains," but he must have a hand or he can not paint a picture; he may feel the rising transport of a dream of sculptured beauty, but his thought can never live in marble without the magic hand. The great organ, strange repository of sweet sounds and celestial harmonies, will not break its silence and can not tell its message to a man with a withered hand. The hand has both an aesthetic and a utilitarian relation to life. It is the most potent factor in the progress and enlightenment, the development and enfranchisement of the human race.

It may be true that "man has been given two hands and one tongue because he ought to do twice as much as he says." At all events, it is safe to say that he needs both hands in a universe where there are

> "So many worlds, so much to do,
>   So little done, such things to be,"

and the tale of the text is doubly sad because the man's *right hand* is withered. Here is a soul with his *best arm* palsied. What a picture of a blemished man!

It is easy to recognize the handicap of a physically withered hand; the discount of a body with a crippled member. According to Paul, there is not only a natural but also a spiritual body. Our experience teaches us that we do not have to die to become conscious of this fact. Every day man's heart beats in two realms. His spiritual organism is invisible, but its proportions are definite and real. Each person is sufficiently acquainted with his own mental, moral, and spiritual weakness to know what it is to have a spiritual body with a withered hand. The man in the synagogue with the limp arm, the worthless hand, the blemished body, is a type of the man whose spiritual life is discounted by defects.

It is impossible for a man with a withered hand to do a sound man's work. The cripple—physical, intellectual, spiritual—has a damaging handicap. Pity the man whose bodily deformity compels him to hobble all the way from the cradle to the grave with crutches! O, the pathos of the intellectual infirmity that makes one stand in the world of thought with a shrunken arm and a shriveled hand! What multitudes of spiritually impotent folk, halt, and maimed, and blind, helplessly waiting for some angel to come and stir the pool! The Church has been too busy nursing cripples to do good work at training soldiers.

Some men are born with withered hands, and some hands wither through lack of use. To whom little is given, of him not much will be required: but woe to him who had a charge and lost his chance. Both earth and heaven are merciful with weakness one can not help, but both abhor the fault that need not be. Let him that knoweth better than he does be sure that his hand is withered. Heaven's greatest grief is not that men have withered hands, but that their blight is self-imposed. Man of the shrunken sinews and dangling, senseless arm, take heart! There is still another chance.

The man who has a withered hand may have his hand made whole. Stretch forth thy hand! Thou canst not? Thy hand has hung there limp too long? Thou wilt not try? Stretch forth thy hand! It takes both God and man to heal a helpless arm. Hast thou a little faith? Canst thou believe? Wilt thou but only try? Stretch forth thy hand! There is a sure specific for a blemished life. It matters not what shrank thy limb. The balm is ready, but thou must do thy part. Stretch forth thy hand! And Christ will make thee whole.

PIOUS IN SPOTS

"Ye tithe mint and rue and every herb, and pass over judgment and the love of God."—*St. Luke xi, 42.*

"True piety bath in it nothing weak, nothing sad, nothing constrained. It enlarges the heart; it is simple, free and attractive."—*Fenelon.*

"Learn to show piety at home."—*1 Timothy v, 4.*

"Measure not men by Sundays, without regarding what they do all the week after."—*Fuller.*

A CAREFUL examination of the life of the average Christian would reveal the fact that he is usually engaged in doing little things which he likes to do and which really cost but little effort. The majority of people know nothing about the dignity of sacrifice. We like to go to church (some of us do), we like to hear good music and sermons, we like to be in the society of good people: but doing as we like may only be the expression of individual prejudices.

We are so fearfully fussy about so many secondary, subordinate, and really non-essential things. Especially is this true in matters religious. It is not at all unlikely that we may be laying great stress upon some little thing as insignificant in the whole realm of duty as the giving of a tenth of the sprigs of mint, and anise, and garden herbs, was in the Master's thought in comparison with "judgment and the love of God." There are people who are wonderfully particular about working their praying-machine who are dreadfully unscrupulous in "the weightier matters of the law." It was the custom of the more accurate Jews to strain all their drinks through linen or gauze, lest unawares they should drink down some little insect and transgress the law. It is fairly possible that we likewise may be riding some little hobby which we have built ourselves, and that, while we are straining out gnats we may be swallowing camels. It is all right to be particular about little sins, but we dare not neglect the great ones.

What is it to be pious? Is the person who prays aloud, groans about his sins, sighs most sadly, lives the most narrow and restricted life, dresses in most plain and unattractive garb, carries a Bible under his arm, and who always is preaching to people, most pious? Not necessarily; in fact, these things are more often the evidence of lack of true piety. Genuine piety is strong; it is simple and happy and free, and graces childhood and old age; it is modest and attractive, the crowning glory of womanhood, and the majestic sweetness of manhood; it is to be filled with soundness and sanity.

Christ never presented a detailed platform of reformation. He concerned Himself with vitalities, and not with accidents and externalities. He never busied Himself in going about patching up broken walls. He simply created a new atmosphere for the soul. His life is the spirit of love, which, when it fills men's hearts, manifests itself in their habits and actions. A truly pious heart is just a good heart living a natural life, sanctifying every rite of worship with the spirit back of the form. A holy heart is simply a whole heart.

The heart that is pious all the way through deals with things in order of their importance and is unceasingly devoted to the spirit instead of the letter. When "judgment and the love of God" rule the understanding and the conscience, mint and rue and all manner of herbs will receive their due attention. Little formalities of worship are of no consequence when the tenor of the life is wrong.

When the soul is sanely, soundly, whole, externalities either of worship or recreation will take care of themselves. True piety is the expression of a condition of rightness and spiritual health. It is never morbid, nor diseased. It lays more stress on essential life than non-essential form. The really pious person is not merely religious in spots. He covets vigor and health of soul. He tries to live at the top of his condition. His religion is his life. He lives it every day, and so his every act becomes an act of worship.

SUNLIGHT AND MOONLIGHT

"I am the light of the world."—*St. John vii, 12.*

"Ye are the light of the world."—*St. Matthew v, 14.*

"Yet the moonlight is the sunlight."—*Tennyson.*

"Moral light is the radiation of the diviner glory."—*Dick.*

"There shall be no night there; and they need no candle, neither light of the sun."—*Revelation xxii, 5.*

"The light of the moon shall be as the light of the sun."—*Isaiah xxx, 26.*

IN a conversation with His disciples concerning a certain blind man whom He had healed, Jesus said to them, "As long as I am in the world, I am the light of the world." But it was contrary to the very nature of things that He should always remain upon the earth. Only for a few brief years could He thus be "the light of the world." Referring to this fact and recognizing His relation to His followers, He continues, "Yet a little while, and the world seeth, Me no more; but ye see Me." He speaks for the coming centuries and lays the responsibility on faithful men in the declaration, "Ye are the light of the world." But they were really only reflectors, and He was still the light. It was as if the Sun were to say to the Moon, "I shall shortly sink beneath the horizon and from the sight of men; but not from yours. Then the only way I shall have of lighting the world will be by shining on your face until men, seeing your glowing cheek shall know that my light still shines. During my absence from the world, O Moon, you must be its light."

There is no light but sunlight. The sun is the luminary and the stars reflectors. Tennyson puts it in poetic phrase, "Yet the moonlight is the sunlight." The sun could not stay in the world by night; if it did, there would be no night. But the sun is never without an agent, though the sky be full of clouds. The moon and the stars and the milky way are proof that the sun is shining. Blessings on the true reflector that gives what light it can! But mighty

Sun, if thou shouldst cease to shine, the day would turn to midnight. O Soul, without the light of God thy night is black and starless!

Without the sunlight there can be no moon-light. Fair Luna has no brightness of her own. Her face grows dark when something blocks the fiery pathway of the sun. Man can not shine with borrowed light with a world thrust in between himself and Christ. Then shun the thing that throws a shadow on thy life, for sometimes the foot-sore traveler walks by night, the kindly Moon his silent guide, and many a soul must climb the steeps to Glory in the light of other lives. Some men will never see the Christ except as they behold His light reflected by those who call themselves or are called by others—Christians. Beware, lest the darkness of thy life may cost some soul its crown.

When the sun and the moon are both in the sky the moon can scarce be seen. When the sun is least apparent the moon may be the fairest, but her beauty is a glory not her own. The moon's chief business is to represent the sunlight; to keep a little candle burning in the night. So men are witnesses for Christ; their little lamp a faint reflection of His light. If the light in them be darkness, they have added to the night. Blessed Christ, Sun of Righteousness, Thou hast said, "He that followeth Me shall not walk in darkness, but shall have the light of life." My life is only a little taper, Lord, but suffer the light on the wick to be a spark from the fiery Sun!

The Lord God is a Sun. He floods the world with light. When the day is done and the sky is dark, He is still the light of life. His glory shines by day and night from the hearts and lives which reflect His light. His light is sunlight and man's light is moonlight. "Yet the moonlight is the sunlight," and he who sees the faintest glimmer gets a gleam of God Himself. Behold the light! The night is past! It is morning!

COLOR BLIND

"Their own wickedness bath blinded them."—(*Apocrypha*) *Wisdom of Solomon xi, 21.*

"Woe unto them that call evil good, and good evil; that put darkness for light, and light for darkness; that put bitter for sweet, and sweet for bitter."—*Isaiah v, 20.*

"Cast out the beam out of thine own eye; and then thou shalt see clearly."—*St. Matthew vii, 5.*

"The Lord openeth the eyes of the blind."—*Psalm cxlvi, 8.*

"The eye observes only what the mind, the heart, the imagination are gifted to see; and sight must be reinforced by insight, before souls can be discerned as well as manners."—*E. P. Whipple.*

"Eyes will not see when the heart wishes them to be blind. Desire conceals truth as darkness does the earth."—*Seneca.*

COLOR-BLINDNESS is the name given to the inability to distinguish separate colors. This physical defect must have ex1sted from time immemorial, though there is no record of the description of a case until the latter part of the eighteenth century, when a man was found who could only distinguish white and black. He could not discern fruit on the trees by its color, but only by its shape. A few years later an English chemist by the name of Dalton gave a description of his own inability to distinguish red from green. This weakness was called "Daltonism" and was only looked upon as one of the strange anomalies of vision. Up till 1818 only two other cases were reported. Within recent years the subject has been sufficiently studied to gain an adequate conception of the percentage of people afflicted with this chromatic defect. Special attention was called to the matter through the investigation of the causes of certain railroad accidents. It appeared that the engineers not only did not, but could not, distinguish the signals of danger which were displayed. Scientific men began an examination of school children, to determine the ratio and grades of defect. The result established the fact that perhaps four per, cent of all males are born color-blind and a little over one per cent of females.

There are in the retina of the eye nerve fibers which are excited by waves of light. The development of color arises from the action of longer or shorter waves upon certain fibers, producing the sensation of a color according to the length of the waves. Long waves excite fibers sensitive to red; medium, those sensitive to green; and short, those sensitive to violet. The absence or paralysis of the nerve-fibers or organs perceiving any one of the primary colors will produce blindness with reference to that color, as red-blindness, green-blindness, violet-blindness. When there is the entire absence of the perception of colors, the eye sees only black and white. There is, therefore, a striking analogy between the laws of physical and spiritual vision. The soul's eye may be totally blind, or it may only be defective and unable to discern lights and shades and colors in the Christian life. The prevailing fault of the human heart is not that it can not see at all, but that it sees "men as trees."

Defective spiritual eye-sight makes it impossible to appreciate all the beauty of the world. Persons thus afflicted are sure to be uncharitable with their fellows. They are devoid of the power which enables them to perceive bright colors and so see only the plainest black and white. Their observations are unjust in proportion as their sight is faulty. They can only assign to others the shades and qualities which they understand themselves. He only sees clearly whose eye is sound and free from motes and beams. The thing seen even takes on the colors of the media through which it is viewed.

Subjective soundness is absolutely necessary to a correct appreciation of objective goodness. When the eye is blinded with wickedness it can not tell good from evil. He who is color-blind and has never seen red, must not doubt its existence, though he can not tell how it looks. God's rainbow of character is made of various hues. What a pity that eyes which only see black and white must bring a world of beauty within the compass of their own conception! O Soul with a blemished eye, you may be loosed of your infirmity! There is a Man who can open eyes that have been blind from the time of birth! There are so many eyes that only see a little of all that might be seen! Lord, open men's eyes and let them see! 'T were a shame to let such glory go to waste! Blind man, look up! and be not faithless but believing.

MAKING FACES

"Be not as the hypocrites, of a sad countenance, for they disfigure their faces."—*St. Matthew vi, 16.*

"A merry heart maketh a cheerful countenance."—*Proverbs xv, 13.*

"A man's wisdom maketh his face to shine."—*Ecclesiastes viii, 1.*

"A wicked man hardeneth his face."—*Proverbs xxi, 29.*

"The show of their countenance doth witness against them."
—*Isaiah iii, 9.*

"We are all sculptors and painters, and our material is our own flesh and blood and bone. Any nobleness begins at once to refine a man's features; any meanness or sensuality to imbrute them."—*Thoreau.*

ALEXANDER SMITH is the author of the statement, "If we could but read it, every human being carries his life in his face, and is good-looking or the reverse, as that life has been good or evil. On our features the fine chisels of thought and emotion are eternally at work."

When "Bobby" Burns, sitting in church behind a proudly-acting and finely-dressed lady, saw a louse crawling all unknown to her upon her hat, and took out his pencil and gave the world these lines,

> "O wad some power the giftie gie us,
> To see oursels as ithers see us,"

he perhaps did not present the finest example of attention to the sermon, but he did declare the subtle truth that if men could see their title pages which others read in face and form, they would not feign to be the thing that they are not. What contortions, deceptions, assumptions, hypocrisies! What posing! What chameleon-like effects! Be not deceived—the world is wise. The lady was not responsible for the presence of the insect on her bonnet, but man is the sculptor of his mien. His very features, though insensibly, come to be formed and to assume their shape and shade from the frequent and habitual expression of the affections of his soul. His character is daily crystallizing in his manners and becoming indelibly imprinted on his face. Whether men know it or not, they are constantly engaged in the business of making faces. Sometimes they make funny faces and the world laughs; sometimes false faces and the world says they lie; sometimes they know not what faces and build them better than they know.

The countenance contains at once a record and a forecast. It is the index of the volume of the past; the foreword of all the future chapters. The face is as legible as a printed page, and no deft skill is needed to read the handwriting of Nature and no superior wisdom to understand her marks. Faces disclose the secrets that the tongue would hide; they tell the tale of wrath and pride, of fear and pain, vexation and contempt, or, peace and joy, respect and faith, or lowliness and love.

It is said that Queen Elizabeth so firmly believed in the fact that the countenance is an index of character, that she often remarked, "A good face is the best letter of recommendation." Who has not felt with Addison, pity for the wife of the man with a sour and shriveled face!

One can not change his title-page and disregard the contents of his life; he can not be externally comely until he is internally right. True beauty is not only the symmetry of external parts; it is the harmony between the outside and the inner life. There is a difference between mere doll-faced beauty and the stronger grace which represents true worth within.

The spiritual nature finds expression in the face. The ideas one delights in are written on his visage; he can not live ignobly and have a noble mien. When the light inside is darkness, the countenance can not shine; when the heart is true and upright, the face will not deny it. Heaven deliver us from the pinched, pointed, withered, wizzened, soured, shriveled, brazen, bilious, cross, critical countenance which tells of the starvation of a spirit feeding on the husks of life when there is a feast in the Father's house! A beneficent soul will have the face of beauty. All culture tells. When the soul is full of the light of love, the countenance will shine with "the glory of God in the face of Jesus Christ."

WEAK SPOTS

"Be watchful, and strengthen the things that remain, that are ready to die; for I have not found thy works perfect before God."
—*Revelation iii, 2.*

"My strength fails because of mine iniquity."—*Psalm xxxi, 10.*

"Not that I have already attained, or am already made perfect; but I press on.... One thing I do.... I press on toward the goal."—*Paul.*

"In all our weaknesses we have one element of strength if we recognize it. Here, as in other things, knowledge of danger is often the best means of safety."—*E. P. Roe.*

"The more weakness, the more falsehood; strength goes straight; every cannon-ball that has in it hollows and holes goes crooked. Weaklings must lie."—*Richter.*

A GENTLEMAN engaged in the manufacture of automobiles stated that he had driven his touring-car five thousand miles and that he had then sent it to the shop, where it was being taken apart to be examined for weak spots. He said "I am going to strengthen the parts which are showing signs of weakness." He was proceeding in the belief that the only way to construct a machine perfect throughout was to strengthen the weak spots until there were none. The investigation would probably reveal the fact that the greater part of the machine was in perfect working order, but the weak place, however small, will damage its efficiency.

The character which man is constructing out of the raw material God has given him is not a machine, but it has weak spots before it has run many miles. It is, therefore, a good thing, once in a while, for one to take his character apart and to examine it that he may reconstruct it, leaving the weak spots out or at least trying to make them stronger. There is more good than bad in almost any person, but in all there are liable to be weak spots which are not only annoying but which cause the character to wabble and to fail to run true. The careless farmer leaves his machinery out in the field exposed to all sorts of weather, and when he wants to use it finds it in bad repair; some folks treat their souls that way.

The best lives have weak spots. Paul had them. They may mean one's downfall if he do not look after them in time. The strain is always on the weakest spot. A character may have but a single flaw, but it really is no stronger than the weak place in it. A chain always breaks at the weakest link. A neglected character, like a neglected machine, will find its weak spots multiplying and becoming weaker if they be not looked after promptly.

Every time one strengthens a weak spot in his character, he fortifies his life. The fewer blemishes within the heart, the greater the resistance against temptation. It is not always easy to discover the exact defect, and some imperfections are harder to remedy than others on account of the relation they bear to the whole. A very small fault will sometimes cause a very great disaster. Life can only be kept in good repair by constant watchfulness and attention to detail.

In the matter of building a character, man is not obliged to invent any part or to experiment on the best method of constructing a life complete. He has a perfect model. He has only to see that/each part is made just like the pattern, and it will not only fit, but be the best. The great Architect of the perfect plan and Master Builder of the perfect work will help man make a perfect imitation. Whose heart is full of flaws must bear the fault himself.

God does not expect of any man that he shall be so perfect that no critic could find a single fault in him, but He does expect him to strive with all the passion of his soul to rid himself of weak spots. Some of God's men and women have been out of repair so long that they are well-nigh consumed with rust, and rot ten with decay. O, Soul, discounted by defects, search out thyself and strengthen the things which remain and are ready to die, for thy works are not found perfect!

CLEAN DIRT

"There is nothing from without a man, that entering into him can defile him, but the things which come out of him, those are they which defile him."—*St. Mark vii, 16.*

"Dirt is not dirt, but only something in the wrong place."—*Palmerton.*

"'Ignorance,' says Ajax, 'is a painless evil.' So I should think is dirt, considering the merry faces that go along with it."—*George Eliot.*

"What hands are here? ha! they pluck out mine eyes.
Will all great Neptune's ocean wash this blood
Clean from my hands? No, this my hand will rather
The multitudinous seas incarnadine."—*Macbeth.*

"Here's the smell of the blood still;
All the perfumes of Arabia will not sweeten this little hand."
—*Lady Macbeth.*

THE philosopher defines dirt as "misplaced matter." Though his definition may be correct, dirt under ordinary circumstances is disagreeable. There is no defense for physical uncleanness, except for that grime which is often the necessary attendant of honest toil. There are places where men must labor in dust-laden and smoke-filled atmospheres until their faces are black and their clothes are soiled, but where the white flower of their manhood may remain unsmirched. This sort of defilement might be called clean dirt.

There is a dirt for which the other name is filth. It is the natural result and sure mark of laziness. It is not gotten from work, but from the failure to work. It is a boon-companion of sloth and indolence, and is always an associate of that poverty which arises from lack of thrift. It is never excusable, and is the first step in the downward road that leads to crime. Dirt, disease, wretchedness, and sin are companionable fellows, and are liable to be found in the same abode. Respectable poor people are always clean.

> "The cottage was a thatched one,
>   The outside old and mean,
> But everything within that cot
>   Was wondrous neat and clean."

Clean dirt is not only dirt that will wash off, but dirt that is unavoidably on. Cleanliness is next to godliness, and there is no apology for uncleanness while water is abundant and soap is cheap. The grime of work and the dust of play are only "misplaced matter." Such dirt is not hard to wash away. It leaves no stain that hurts.

> "A pair of dimpled, dirty hands
>   The lad brings home when through with play,
> But mother never scolds, because
>   Clean dirt is quickly washed away.
>
> "The barefoot lad brings dusty feet,
>   For he has journeyed far today,
> But mother bathes them pink and sweet;
>   Clean dirt's not hard to wash away.
>
> "God keep the little feet from soil
>   Of evil paths in life, and may
> The hands be stained alone by toil;
>   Clean dirt like that will wash away."

It is possible to be physically clean and morally unclean. Dirt that will wash off is bad enough, but clean beside the dirt that water can not cleanse. There is nothing quite so wretched as a heart that is soiled with sin. Practical impiety of life proceeds from such a state; the influence of such a soul is bad. The dangerous tempter is the one that looks all right, but really is all wrong. What an incongruity—face and hands washed clean with water, and a heart besmirched and filthy! What symmetry of beauty—clean hands and a heart all pure!

The filthy heart can not be cleansed with water. There is not water enough in the ocean to wash the stain from an unclean heart. The sad experiences of Macbeth and his Lady both illustrate this fact. The guilty heart must be purged with blood. So deep is the taint of sin that mere washing will not suffice. The clean heart must be a new heart; no bleaching of the old one is enough. The ancient Singer felt the need when his soul cried out, "Create in me a clean heart." No one but God can cleanse a life and keep it clean and pure.

The face may be dirty and the garments soiled, and yet the heart be clean as the lotus-lily that springs from the black muck-bed; the hands may be white and the face perfumed, and the heart still black within. O, Soul, it is false to be fair without until you are fair within! Only the white-souled and clean of heart shall ever live with God. Are you clean in every part?

THE HOUSE BY THE SIDE OF THE ROAD

"The Son of man . . . a friend of publicans and sinners."
—*St. Matthew xi, 19.*

"We should live soberly, righteously, and godly in this present world."—*Titus ii, 12.*

"He was a friend to man, and he lived in a house by the side of the road."—*Homer.*

THERE are two classes of people who have always refused to come into intimate relations with the common people in everyday life—the religious ascetic who is afraid of being contaminated, and the aristocratic fool who thinks himself too fine. The secluded cloisters of gloomy monasteries, with their dark cells and dismal retreats, and the pale recluse with his sad countenance and somber dress bear testimony to a superstitious fanaticism at best poorly representing the character of Him who spent a busy life in contact with the people; while opulent villas and suburban mansions, with walled gardens and embowered lanes, and the rock-bound castle with gilded turret and massive arch, speak of the social barriers which divide the so-called lowly from the so-called great.

The influence of the professional religionist is and always has been bad. When one separates himself from society and the affairs of men to practice a negative religion, he misinterprets God's word, "Come ye out from among them and be ye separate," which means a separateness from the spirit of worldliness and not from worldly people. The Christian religion was intended by its Author to be a practical, positive, active force in the world, though in principle not of it. He is most truly Christlike who, instead of shutting himself away from the surging, fetid stream of human life, plunges in and with the strength of manly purpose rescues perishing souls. The world yearns for the exemplification of Christian character in real men—men who live "soberly, righteously, and godly" in a world of actual things. Christian men and ministers serve the Kingdom best when they mingle with the crowd on the highway of life, the incarnation of manliness, virtue, and godly fear. There is something uncanny about a skirted priest; something irresistible about the sound goodness of a man. The haughty spirit that shuns the thronging highway on account of the supposed pre-eminence of wealth or name, is not only non-Christian, but ill-becoming to a man. God looks on hearts and not on robes and not on wealth nor worldly wisdom, and His best servant lives in a house by life's most populous and busy roadside and is a friend to man.

> "There are hermit souls that live withdrawn,
>   In the place of their self-content;
> There are souls like stars, that live apart
>   In a fellowless firmament;
> There are pioneer souls that blaze their path
>   Where highway never ran—
> But let me live by the side of the road,
>   And be a friend to man.
>
> "Let me live in a house by the side of the road,
>   Where the race of men go by—
> The men who are good and the men who are bad!
>   As good and as bad as I.
> I would not sit in the scorner's seat,
>   Nor hurl the cynic's ban.
> Let me live in a house by the side of the road,
>   And be a friend of man.
>
> "I see from my house by the side of the road,
>   By the side of the highway of life,
> The men who press with the ardor of hope,
>   The men who are faint with strife.
> But I turn not away from their smiles nor their tears—
>   Both parts of an infinite plan—
> Let me live in my house by the side of the road,
>   And be a friend to man."

The test of the Christian faith must ever be found in the drudgery, the hum-drum, the hot, dusty stretches of the highway of life. Man's religion must be a practical, everyday affair, as much a part of his make-up as his lungs and blood. He who would exemplify his Master's spirit must recognize the fact that the difference between men is one of heart and not of houses. To be a friend of man is to be a friend of God. True religion is a sound, sane, pure, manly mode of life in the very presence of evil and among men, whether good or bad. If the Christian life mean a sober, righteous, godly living; if it mean to be a man at his highest and his best, then count me with Christians. If by befriending my fellow-man I can be a friend of God, then let me dwell by the side of the road and be a friend to man.

THE BACK YARD

"Clear thou me from hidden faults."—*Psalm xix, 12. (R. V.)*

"There is nothing covered that shall not be revealed; and nothing hid that shall not be known."—*St. Matthew x, 26.*

"No man, for any considerable period, can wear one face to himself and another to the multitude, without finally getting bewildered as to which may be true."—*Hawthorne.*

"Were we to take as much pains to be what we ought, as we do to disguise what we are, we might appear like ourselves without being at the trouble of any disguise at all."—*Rochefoucauld.*

"Of all the evil spirits abroad in the world, insincerity is the most dangerous."—*Froude.*

The subject was suggested to the writer while looking through the window of a train which was backing into the union depot past the rear of a number of lots fronting on a very attractive street of a certain city. The appearance of the residences evidently depended very much on whether one had a front or a back view. The prospect from the rear was anything but attractive. There was a conglomerate disarrangement of rubbish, and lumber, and dirt, such as the passer-by on the street never would have dreamed could be the background of so fair a front. Side by side with the lots in question were others so tidy and neat that the rear could have exchanged places with the front without damage to the attractiveness of the street.

Now all this is a parable which teaches that there are two views of life—the front and the rear. The lots with rubbish in the back yard are types of duplicity and sham; the ones with rear and front equally clean are symbols of openness and sincerity. When the Psalmist uttered the text he had in mind what might be termed in homely language, the back yard of life. He knew that a thing to be really clean must be all clean; he prayed for deliverance from the sins which are kept in the background; he yearned for a heart that would not only look fair, but bear investigation. The subject is only another way of saying "hidden faults and secret sins."

People whose back yards will not bear inspection usually try to interest visitors in the front view. All this is folly, for the time spent exhibiting the disguise might be sufficient to set the whole house in order; besides, such persons must live in constant fear lest somebody back in past the rear some time. The hypocrite lives in guilty dread that his mask will be found out. As long as he is conscious that there is trash upon his premises, he is ill at ease in the presence of one whose yard is clean. As a consequence he begins to dodge and skulk and to avoid the man of open heart. One is known by the company he keeps.

It is impossible for any man to be at peace with God the background of whose character is polluted with sin. Jesus pronounced His most scathing anathemas against hypocrisy. If the Almighty is ever intolerant it must be with him whose heart does not ring true; whose soul is filled with dark deeds and secret sin. The outside counts for little when the inside is unclean. It is possible to fool the world for a little while, but before God appraises the value of a man, He walks all around the lot.

The character that is not equally fair on all sides needs a cleaning up. The first thing necessary toward the beautifying of a garden is to clear the ground of trash; then comes both care and cultivation and the planting of the seeds, the growths from which shall afterward adorn it The first prayer the heart should make is, "Clear thou me from hidden faults," but let that heart remember that God will move no refuse that the soul can oust itself. Paul must plant and Apollos must water before God can give the increase. The first act in working out one's own salvation is to cart away the rubbish from the back yard of his life.

It is worth while to be clean clear through. A complete renovation may be necessary to make the heart a place where God delights to dwell. O, Soul, sick with secret sin, look unto God; He is the health of thy countenance! Thy clothing can only be of wrought gold when thou art all glorious within. When thy heart is clean and thy spirit right the garden of thy life will be the Paradise of God.

STRAYED SHEEP

"All we, like sheep, have gone astray; we have turned every one to his own way; and the Lord bath laid on him the iniquity of us all."
—*Isaiah liii, 6.*

"If a man have an hundred sheep and one of them be gone astray, doth he not leave the ninety and nine, and go into the mountains, and seek that which is gone astray?"—*St. Matthew xviii, 12.*

"My people have been lost sheep; their shepherds have caused them to go astray, they have turned them away on the mountains; they have gone from mountain to hill, they have forgotten their resting place."
—*Jeremiah i, 6.*

"I am the good shepherd, and know my sheep and am known of mine."—*St. John x, 14.*

"Away on the mountains wild and bare,
Away from the tender Shepherd's care."

ONE of the most beautiful figures in the Bible is that which represents the Lord as shepherd and His people as sheep. A good shepherd knows his Sheep by name and misses even one when anything has happened to it. There is a sense in which with respect to the heart it is a compliment to man to be likened to a sheep. There is a certain kindness in the statement, "All we like sheep have gone astray." It is as if our wandering were due more to ignorance of what were best than a wilful desire to do what Ought not to be done. And yet, when the Prophet says, "We have turned every one to his own way," there is a suggestion that the sheep feels that he knows better than the shepherd where he can find the most satisfying pasturage and turns to *choose* his own way. Stupidity that leads to destruction is bad enough, but, O, the criminality of the *choice* that deliberately turns toward death!

Strayed is a mild word. It does not indicate wilfulness so much as an easy-going indifference. It suggests a *gradual* separation from the flock. At first the wanderer seems to be at a safe distance; it can see and hear the shepherd and the rest of the flock: but little by little the distance increases, and when the day is done there is a sheep lost in the darkness where it is subject to the mercy of wild beasts of prey. There are many directions in which the sheep may stray. The danger is universal. There is a significance in that word "all" that touches every one. Some of the wanderers are still within sound of the Shepherd's voice, and some have gone so far that they can not even see Him. O, how blessed to know that the Good Shepherd will seek out the lost ones and carry them back!

Lost sheep always begin by straying; no sheep ever tried to lose himself. Straying is dangerous business; before they know it, the sheep have gone farther than they thought. No man ever set out to be a hardened sinner. No soul deliberately loses itself. The road to perdition branches from the way of righteousness by an angle so small that the traveler may not realize for some time that he is really off the track, but once on the by-path every step takes him farther from the path that leads to life. The danger point is where sin is all but imperceptible. All that a soul needs to do to become lost is simply to stray.

The attitude of the Good Shepherd toward the sheep which have strayed is tender and beautiful. He goes into the desert and over rough places to find them. He is more anxious about the lost ones than the ones which have never strayed. When He finds the poor, bleating, shivering, starving weakling, He takes it in His arms and carries it in His bosom. O, Soul, you who have strayed only to the out skirts of the green pastures, Listen! Beyond are desert sands and rocky hills and perilous steeps and ravenous beasts. Stay, then, within sight of the Shepherd and within hearing of His voice. He will lead you into fresh fields of tender pasture, and cause you to lie down beside waters of restful peace. Thou shalt not want. O, Soul, thou who hast strayed far, far beyond the Shepherd's call, "sick and helpless and ready to die," cry out if only feebly, for it may be the Shepherd shall pass that way and hear thy voice and take thee home again!

THEORY AND PRACTICE

"Having a form of godliness, but denying the power thereof."
—*2 Timothy iii, 5.*

"Pure religion and undefiled before our God and Father is this, to visit the fatherless and widows in their affliction, and to keep himself unspotted from the world."—*St. James i, 27.*

"If to do were as easy as to know what were good to do, chapels had been churches, and poor men's cottages princes' palaces. It is a good divine that follows his own instructions; I can easier teach twenty what were good to be done than be one of the twenty to follow mine own instructions."—*"Portia," in "Merchant of Venice."*

"Most men take least notice of what is plain, as if that were of no use; but puzzle their thoughts and lose themselves in those vast depths and abysses which no human understanding can fathom."—*Sherlock.*

THESE are days when purity is at a premium. We hear a great deal about pure food laws and of investigation of fraud and misrepresentation. The ban of public contempt is on all adulteration. The spirit of reformation is in the air and the gospel of commercial honesty is being proclaimed from the altar of the executive mansion and the hearthstone of the lowliest cottager, and please God, the day is not far distant when civic unrighteousness shall become so loathsome that it will be cast out forever from the business transactions of men. So long as business is tainted, religion is bound to be corrupted. If the one goes down it drags the other with it. The test for purity must, therefore, include religion, and the basis of the inquiry into man's relations with his Maker must ever be found in the practical affairs of life.

The standard by which purity is tested is not relative, but absolute. Quality must reach a certain definite degree before it is pure. This is as true of religion as of anything else which it is possible to adulterate. There are certain rules by which a chemical analysis can be made, but the only way to get at a man's religion to apply the test is to take a piece of his life and reduce it to its elements. One thing is certain, that his religion can not rise above the spirit which dominates his business life. Pure religion is a practical thing. The religion condemned by prophets and stigmatized by the Savior is the religion of form and unpracticed theories.

To lay stress on the form and to deny the power is to mistake religiousness for religion. The former is only a susceptibility to the mystic elements of religion, especially religious feeling apart from its duties; the latter is a belief *binding* the spiritual nature of man to a super natural Being on whom he is conscious that he is dependent, and is the *practice* that springs out of such a relation. The religion of too many people is a theory that they never have tried to practice. The religious theorist always insists that others shall conform to his self-invented standards.

The dogmas of men sometimes differ from the doctrines of God. A Church member is not always a Christian. The denominational bigot is always a Pharisee. The practice of religion establishes doctrines based upon experience. He only understands the doctrine of Repentance who has repented. The doctrine of Divine Sonship is established when some poor soul can feel that God accepts his service and that he is His child. The hard thing is not to know what to do, but to do what we know. An ounce of practice is worth a ton of theory. Faith, if it hath not works, is dead. One shows his faith by his works. Soul, thy religion is vain if thou art only theoretically related to God! What thou dost to thy brother man is as if it were done to God. The test of a man's religion is in his works and life.

HOLDING FAST

"That which ye have already hold fast till I come. He that overcometh, and keepeth My works unto the end, to him will I give power."
—*Revelation ii, 25, 26.*

"The conditions of conquest are always easy. We have but to toil awhile, endure awhile, believe always, and never turn back."—*Simms.*

"Hold that fast which thou hast, that no man take thy crown. Him that overcometh will I make a pillar in the temple of my God."
—*Revelation iii, 11, 12.*

"If a man has any brains at all, let him hold on to his calling, and, in the grand sweep of things, his turn will come at last."—*W. McCune.*

"He that shall endure unto the end, the same shall be saved."
—*St. Matthew xxiv, 13.*

IF greatness could be obtained by a single effort, no one would be unwilling to pay the price. But greatness does n't often come suddenly, and when it does it does n't often stay. Success in any line is achieved by holding fast to what one has and by working for dear life for a little more; by keeping at it and by never giving up—the name for such a method is per severance.

If perfection of heart could be gotten in a day or purchased at a bargain counter, no one would be without it. But perfection doesn't fall from the skies; it lies at the top of a sun-crowned hill and is reached by a roadway difficult and steep. So much time is required to reach its heights that many a soul, like Moses, has died in sight of the promised land. Happy is he who once in a while gets a glimpse of the hill-top; who holds his own and climbs a little higher every day, for the will is taken for the deed and to be reaching for the prize counts the same as if one reached it. To be God's man, to hold fast what one has, and to be faithful unto death, is to have a vantage ground from which one may step clear into heaven, whether his grave be on the mountain top or on the mountain side.

With reference to the higher things in life men are usually exhorted to get, but this text advises them to keep. It suggests a possibility of losing what one already has, if he be not careful. It hints at the necessity of defensive warfare lest another take one's crown. Getting religion is important, but keeping it is equally so. The moment one resolves on a life of righteousness he enters a contest in which Evil challenges his right to his crown every step of the way. The most dangerous enemy is a thief. One is not half so liable to have his virtue wrested from him as stolen.

The godly life must be one of continual watchfulness. The righteous man must have a guard on duty all the time. The tourist who visits the home of the President of France finds a guard stationed at each corner of the walled enclosure surrounding the house; it is a guarded dwelling! Man is obliged to set a watch-tower at the outposts of his very heart to protect it against the inroads of unwelcome guests.

> "My soul be on thy guard,
>   Ten thousand foes arise,
> The hosts of sin are pressing hard,
>   To draw thee from the skies."

The crown is only for the one who endures unto the end and is faithful. Perseverance always wins the race, as many a parable teaches. It is told of King Bruce, the founder of the Scottish monarchy, that once when greatly discouraged and about to give up the idea of freeing Scotland from the English, he and some of his men took refuge in a barn. As he sat there thinking of impending defeat, he saw a spider trying to fasten his web to a beam. Twelve times the insect tried, but did not give up, and the thirteenth time succeeded. It was enough; King Bruce had learned his lesson, and he arose and tried until he drove the enemy from his country. Even greater was the lesson Timour learned when he saw the ant attempt to climb a wall with a load much larger than itself. Sixty-nine times it tried and failed, but the seventieth time it conquered. God helps saints who persevere. An Indian who had caught the genius of a faithful life sang his conviction in this simple verse:

> "Go on, go on, go on, go on,
>   Go on, go on, go on,
> Go on, go on, go on, go on,
>   Go on, go on, go on."

One must be sure even of his last step. It is not enough to be faithful in spots and at some times. One must be steadfast; he must hold fast to the goodness which he already has. It is a common fault to be very zealous for a little time and then gradually to lose enthusiasm. The world needs men who "hold out faithful." Too many persons are like the boy who was studying a lesson that required some time. He began in earnest and for a while was all-absorbed. But a bright-colored butterfly came flitting by, and he closed his book and began to chase the insect. How easily one may be turned from his real purpose! Beware! Hast thou a little faith? Hold it fast! "To him that overcometh and keepeth My works to the end, will I give power," saith the Lord, your God.

> "Ne'er think the victory won,
>   Nor lay thine armor down:
> The work of faith will not be done
>   Till thou obtain the crown."

SOUR GRAPES

"What mean ye, that ye use this proverb concerning the land of Israel, saying, The fathers have eaten sour grapes, and the children's teeth are set on edge?"—*Ezekiel xviii, 2*.

"The most important thought I ever had was that of my individual responsibility to God."—*Daniel Webster*.

"It is nowhere said either in the Old Testament or the New that God visits the iniquities of the fathers upon the children, except where the children obstinately persist in imitating the iniquities of the fathers."
—*Wordsworth*.

"All souls are Mine ... the soul that sinneth, it shall die; but if a man be just and do that which is lawful and right ... he shall surely live."—*The Word of God*.

THE text is the statement of a popular proverb that had gained currency in the later years of the kingdom of Judah. This theory of retribution had taught that the sin of a father could be transmitted to his son, and that the child, therefore, was often punished by Providence for the guilt of his parent. Previous to the time of Ezekiel the family or tribe was looked upon as a unity whose individual members were involved in the actions of the head. So the whole family of Achan is made to perish for the sin of their father; and the sons of Saul expiated their father's crime long after he was dead. It was the conviction of the Jews that the calamity of the captivity was due to the sins of Manasseh. They therefore excused themselves from blame on the ground that the sins for which they suffered were not their own.

The prophet here breaks with the idea that the fate of the child is necessarily dependent upon the deeds of the parent. This setting aside of the supposed truth of the prevalent proverb is Ezekiel's most characteristic contribution to theology. He introduced the thought that God does not deal with men *en masse*, but individually, and that each man's destiny corresponds to his own character regardless of what may or may not have been his family antecedents.

The teaching of the proverb was not in harmony with natural law. In the realm of nature and of fact if a man eat sour grapes his own are the teeth to be set on edge. In the moral sphere, according to the proverb, a man might eat sour grapes throughout his life and bring upon himself no evil, while the consequence of his sinful life might fall upon his children. Our sense of justice rebels at such a thought as that. We, in the light of the clearer day, can not help but feel that each individual stands in immediate relation to God; that this position gives man independent personal worth; and that one's destiny depends upon his own free actions.

Each individual is responsible for his own acts, and for his alone. He is consequently rewarded according to his merit. So far as his relation to the past is concerned he is under the obligation of living up to his ancestry if it were good, and of redeeming it if it were bad.

"He that doeth righteousness is righteous" is the sum of Ezekiel's teaching. The soul that sinneth shall die, even though it be the scion of a godly parentage. Eternal justice will be meted out on the basis of what men have done and the principles which have governed their lives.

After God's method of dealing with folks, the old proverb would have to say that the person who eats sour grapes will find his own teeth set on edge. The curse of the life of a sinful parent may overshadow the life of his child and the blessing of a worthy sire fall like a benediction on his offspring, but the fact still remains that neither guilt nor virtue can ever be transmitted. One either stands or falls on the virtues or defects of his individual soul. Personality has a divine significance. Each man must answer for himself to God and each will receive his own reward.

PAYING BACK

"Say not, I will do so to him as he hath done to me."—*Proverbs xxiv, 29.*

"By taking revenge a man is but even with his enemy; but in passing over it he is superior."—*Bacon.*

"Ye have heard that it bath been said, An eye for an eye and a tooth for a tooth; but I say unto you, Resist not evil."—*St. Matthew v, 38, 39.*

"He who has injured thee was either stronger or weaker than thyself. If weaker, Spare him, if stronger, Spare thyself."—*Seneca.*

"Render to no man evil for evil."—*Romans xii, 17 (R. V.)*

The statement of St. Augustine that "The command, thou shalt give life for life, eye for eye, tooth for tooth, was not given to excite the fires of hatred but to restrain them," helps to a clear interpretation of the text. It was not an urging to "get even," but a demand that one should not any more than "get even." Revenge has never been satisfied with repaying only as much injury as it has received. This law, then, was for the purpose of setting a limit on immoderate and unjust vengeance. It is a forward step. It is justice asserting itself by saying, "You have a right to do unto others as others have done unto you, but in nowise shall the injury returned be greater than the wrong received—it shall be only eye *for* eye, tooth *for* tooth."

The author of the Proverbs, anticipating the morality of the Sermon on the Mount, announces the higher law of Mercy which declares, "Thou shalt not return any injury for wrongs received, but thou shalt *forgive* and return good for evil." Justice is better than unbridled license, but mercy is an attribute of God Himself. The crowning precept of the advancing scale is Love. It is bad to be unjust; it is good to be just and to give no more injury than we get; it is better to be merciful and to forgive; it is best to love your enemies, to do good to those who hate you, and to pray for those who despitefully use you and persecute you.

It seems that there has always and everywhere been in human nature an elemental hate that takes a sort of fiendish delight in the misfortune of enemies. The Psalmist speaking of those who had compassed him about said, "Let burning coals fall upon them; let them be cast into the fire; into the deep pit that they rise not again." Even Jeremiah could say of his enemies, "Lord, Thou knowest all their counsel against me to slay me; forgive not their iniquity, neither blot out their sin from Thy sight; but let them be overthrown before Thee; deal Thou with them in the time of Thine anger." Still, men seem to delight in the downfall of rivals; still, the act of vengeance is performed, the bitter retort given, the abusive letter written; still, men resort to all kinds of meanness to "get even" and to "pay back." My soul, do not usurp thy Maker's place! Vengeance belongs to God. It is not thy prerogative to "pay back."

The soul never appears so strong; never enjoys such satisfying delight; never so thoroughly overcomes all opposition as when it foregoes revenge and dares to forgive an injury. The happiness of revenge is a diabolical happiness. Kindness will completely overcome an enemy and often change him to a friend. In an atmosphere of pity personal resentment always dies. No one who realizes how much there is to pity in the world can have a place for vengeful feelings. Whittier has touchingly set the truth in these pathetic lines:

> "My heart was heavy, for its trust had been
> Abused, its kindness answered with foul wrong;
> So turning gloomily from my fellow-men,
> One summer Sabbath-day I strolled among
> The green mounds of the village burying place;
> Where pondering how all human love and hate
> Find one sad level; and how soon or late,
> Wronged and wrong-doer, each with meekened face,
> And cold hands folded over a still heart,
> Pass the green threshold of a common grave,
> Whither all footsteps tend, whence none depart,
> Awed for myself, and pitying my race,
> Our common sorrow, like a mighty wave,
> Swept all my pride away, and, trembling, I forgave."

Man's duty of forgiveness is based upon his need of God's forgiveness. He who does not forgive his fellows need not expect God's pardon. General

Oglethorpe once said to Wesley, "I never forgive." "Then, I hope, sir," said Wesley, "you never sin." Only the brave know how to forgive. How rare the souls which can say, "Father, forgive them, for they know not what they do!" Little hearts hold grudges and pay back dirt. Great hearts live above the vice of vengeance in the calm fellowship of their regnant Lord. "Overcome evil with good."

LIFE FILLED FULL

"I came not to destroy, but to fulfill."—*St. Matthew v, 17*.

(NOTE.—The Greek infinitive, "plerosai," translated in both the authorized and revised versions, "to fulfill," means when literally translated, "to fill or make full; to satisfy; to complete." A very suggestive translation of the text might therefore be, *"I came not to destroy, but to fill full."*)

"Till we all come in the unity of the faith, and of the knowledge of the Son of God, unto a perfect man, unto the measure of the stature of the fullness of Christ."—*Ephesians iv, 13*.

"For this cause I bow my knees unto the Father of our Lord Jesus Christ, . . . that ye, being rooted and grounded in love, may be able to comprehend with all saints what is the breadth, and length, and depth, and height; and to know the love of Christ that passeth knowledge, that ye might be filled with all the fullness of God."—*Ephesians iii, 14, 17-19*.

THERE has always been in the world a great deal of unintelligent prejudice against the kingdom of God. Christ was not understood by His contemporaries. One of the first things the Son of man was called upon to do was to correct misconceptions of Himself and His office. Many people still hold erroneous ideas of what is meant by being His followers. When the Savior came He found that the people had deified the law and the prophets. They only knew the false and unsatisfying peace of ritual. They were laboriously trying to make their way to heaven by keeping the letter of the commandments and at the same time neglecting mercy, judgment, and truth. They did not seem able to grasp the thought that a principle can govern action. They had to have a literal regulation covering each specific deed or problem. They therefore thought that Jesus was about to do away with the law when He announced a few declarations which He said embraced the whole realm of conduct. Many Christians today are so enslaved by the letter that they must have a rule for every little act of life. O,

Soul, enter the larger freedom! Get the spirit of Christ within and then do what seemeth good!

The religion of Christ destroys nothing worth saving. It makes the individual conscience the judge of what is worth the while, but it does demand an intelligent decision. Its purpose is ever to enlarge one's usefulness and to amplify his powers. When the spirit of the Master comes into a life it enriches every worthy element in it. It fulfills it as the noon the dawn. The noon is dawn filled full of sunlight. It fulfills it as the man the child. Manhood is childhood filled full. Christlikeness is life at its best.

One ought to be concerned about the con tents of his life. A life filled with rubbish is worse than an empty life. It is impossible to fill a life with good things until it be emptied of the bad. What a pity that some souls will not suffer the trash to be cleared away! They would not feel at home if their hearts were clean. Christ came to cleanse man's heart and then to fill it full. O, the wealth of a life that God endows! Love is affluent! It has everything and abounds.

The Christian faith teaches the measure of a full-grown man. It stands for the completest possible maturity of the physical, mental, and moral powers of life. Its business is not to make men narrow but truly broad; it would have them know good whenever and wherever they see it and to comprehend the all-expansiveness of the mercy of the Lord. It seeks to fill life full of right.

A life filled full is a life symmetrical, rich in worthy achievement, grand in lofty purposes, and complete in healthy wholeness. It is sane, settled, balanced, fixed. It is truly holy because truly whole. It is the life God meant His child to live. You can never be full-grown till your life is filled clear full. No one but God can ever fill it full. He is ready now. Are you?

THE FRATERNITY OF SORROW

"That I may know Him . . . and the fellowship of His suffering."
—*Philippians iii, 10.*

"There is no flock, however watched and tended,
But one dead lamb is there!
There is no fireside, howsoe'er defended,
But has one vacant chair!"
—*Longfellow.*

"Our light affliction, which is but for a moment, worketh for us a far more exceeding and eternal weight of glory."—*2 Corinthians iv, 17.*

"Never morning wore to evening but some heart did break."
—*Tennyson.*

"There shall be no more death, neither sorrow, nor crying, neither shall there be any more pain."—*Revelation xxi, 4.*

IT is not wise, either for the sake of self or others, to nurse our grief or harp upon our sorrows. Melancholy is the result of brooding over troubles, and pessimism comes from thinking wholly on the ills of life. On the other hand, it ought to be said that the mere thinking on health and soundness does not destroy the fact of pain; that an assumed cheerfulness may only cover a hidden canker; and that the divinest optimism is often only the fruit of a courage strong enough to keep sweet in spite of bitterness, failure, and loss.

It is well sometimes to look life squarely in the face; to behold its portrait in the somber hues; to see the shades as well as lights, and to get if possible the right perspective. In the presence of the picture unembellished, we grow sympathetic and feel the bond that binds us to our fellow-man; we behold ourselves as we view others; we seem to become a part of earth's joys and sacrifice, its triumphs and its blessed hopes. It is well that we should

"Share our mutual woes,
Our mutual burdens bear."

We dare not overlook the fact that life has cares and anxieties, burdens and trials, and the saddest part of it all is that they are not the exception, but the rule.

It is none the less true, though we fain would forget it, that "never morning wore to evening but some heart did break;" and that

> "There is no flock, however watched and tended,
>   But one dead lamb is there!
> There is no fireside, howsoe'er defended,
>   But has one vacant chair!"

In the face of the indubitable evidence of observation and experience we are under the necessity of acknowledging that we belong to the fellowship of pain and that we are members of the fraternity of sorrow. There are no eyes which have not wept, no hearts which have not bled; there are no shoulders which have not borne burdens, no feet which were never tired nor weary; there is no life entirely free from pain, and no soul which does not carry some load of grief. We do not live long until we wear a crown of thorns, nor go far until we come to Calvary. We belong to a fellowship of suffering.

Sorrow is a part of the great school or scheme by which God trains and strengthens our hearts. The Priest said to Evangeline after she had sought long and patiently for Gabriel and had refused to give up the quest:

> "Sorrow and silence are strong, and patient endurance is godlike.
> Therefore accomplish thy labor of love, till thy heart is made godlike,
> Purified, strengthened, perfected, and rendered more worthy of heaven."

The soul's refinement and glory depend upon its triumphant passage through fire and flood. Martyrdom in the eyes of the world looks like failure, but it shall not go without its reward. It will be worth while to belong to the white-robed throng concerning whom it shall be said, "These are they which came out of great tribulation." There is a sense in which one may actually glory in tribulation. We are refined by the tests of life.

> "Then welcome each rebuff
> That turns earth's smoothness rough,
>   Each sting that bids nor sit, nor stand, but go.

> Be thy joy three-parts pain;
> Strive, and hold cheap the strain;
>> Learn, nor account the pang; dare, never grudge the throe."

In our knowledge of trouble and sorrow we find our common lot. No human fortification is proof against the truth of the statement, "The days of our years are three-score years and ten, and if by reason of strength they be four-score years, yet is there strength, labor, and sorrow." The differences between men are largely in the incidents of life and not in the experiences of the heart. There are differences in endowments, and the difficulty is that some men get stuck up over the fact that they have been entrusted with talents and fail to recognize the responsibility of the trust. The bond of brotherhood is always weakened when we emphasize our dissimilarities and fail to note the things we have in common.

There are times when the heart finds great comfort in the fellowship of suffering. "Misery loves company," and the soul craves the sympathy of those who have borne similar burdens and have gone through the heat of the day. Much as it is often prized, human sympathy has its limitations and human help fails beyond a certain point. There are times when every normal man is driven to his knees before God because he feels there is nowhere else to go. It rejoices the heart to know that when all other resources fail, it may find succor in the fellow ship of the one who was "a man of sorrows and acquainted with grief."

The blessedness of knowing Christ is to belong to the fellowship of His suffering as well as to be a partaker of His most blessed peace and joy. He endured the cross; He was made a perfect example for us through suffering. He did not discountenance pain; He groaned with its hurt. He drank the cup of sorrow to its dregs; He became acquainted with earth's trials while knowing heaven's balm. He speaks from the threshold of the Father's house and says to the weary, heavy-laden one, "Come, I will give you rest, and to all grief-rent, bleeding, broken hearts:

> "Come, ye disconsolate, where'er ye languish;
>> Come to the mercy-seat, fervently kneel;
> Here bring your wounded hearts, here tell your anguish;
>> Earth has no sorrow that Heaven can not heal."

I WON'T DO IT

"A certain man had two sons: and he came to the first and said, Son, go work to-day in my vineyard. He answered and said, I will not."
—*St. Matthew xxi, 28, 29.*

"Whatsoever he saith unto you, do it."—*St. John ii, 5.*

"Do God's will as if it were thy will, and He will accomplish thy will as if it were His own."—*Rabbi Gamaliel.*

"God can do nothing when the will is wrong; when you get your will right, you will find that God always has been on your side."
—*Joseph Parker.*

THE text is taken from the parable which represents two sons—one, rude but afterward thoughtful and penitent, and finally obedient; another, polite but afterward thoughtless, insincere, and finally disobedient. The first represents the common sinner; the second, the Pharasaic religionist. The emphasis of the picture is laid on the fact that it is not so much what men *say* as what they *do* that counts. We tremble at the thought of the straightness of the way and the narrowness of the gate when we remember the words, "If the righteous scarcely be saved, where shall the sinner and the ungodly appear?" but, here we are taught that the stubborn sinner that changes his mind and repents and brings forth fruits meet for the same shall enter the kingdom before the professing Christian who makes polite promises and never does anything. The ultimate test which shall try men's lives will be on the basis of what they have done rather than on what they have said.

"I won't do it," is the reply that the sinner makes to God's invitations, and to His command, "Go, work today in My vineyard." He claims to have "reasons" for so doing. He says that he is not ready; that there are hypocrites in the Church; that he is as good as many who profess more. If argued out of his positions and shown that they are only "excuses," he will probably say, "I will, if some one else will." When, however, he gets in earnest and is willing to act on his own initiative, God will honor his con science. Though he be stubborn and disobedient, if he change his mind and repent, the Heavenly Father will forgive him and make his heart as clean as if he had never sinned.

"I won't do it," is the reply of many a Christian to the call of duty. He, too, has certain "reasons" for his reply. He has n't time, he is not capable; he would rather not try than to try and fail; anyway, he has opinions of his own on the matter. O shame! Thrice shame, Christian, to sing, "I'll go where you want me to go; I'll say what you want me to say; I'll do what you want me to do;" and then when the Master says, "Go, work to-day in My vineyard," to reply by actions, if not by word, "I won't do it! God has more respect for the conscienceless sinner than the conscienceless saint. It is better to say, "I won't do it," and then repent, than to say, "I will," and then not keep the promise. The person who has thrashed out the problem of duty until he obeys, on the ground of conscience, is always of some consequence. It is easier to deal with an opponent in open controversy than with the moral coward who agrees and promises and never once fulfills. The Church is damaged by members who say "I will" and act "I won't."

Deeds are better than words. Talk is cheap; work is costly. Both heaven and earth pay premiums for men who talk little and do much. Two architects were candidates for the erection of a temple at Athens. One discoursed at length on different orders of architecture and on how the temple should be built. The other only remarked that what his brother had *spoken* he could do, and was awarded the contract. No person was ever called to be a Christian who did not hear as soon as he listened enough to hear at all, "Go, *work*!" God help the man who says "I will" to do it, and him who says "I won't" to change his mind.

LETTING THE TRUTH SLIP

"Therefore we ought to give the more earnest heed to the things which we have heard, lest at any time we should let them slip."
—*Hebrews ii, 1 (Old Version).*

"Therefore we ought to give the more earnest heed to the things which were heard, lest haply we drift away from them."—*(Revised Version.)*

"Therefore it is necessary for us more earnestly to hold in mind the things heard, lest at some time or other we let them leak out."
—*(Suggestive Translation.)*

NOTE.—"This is a metaphor taken from unstanch vessels ; the staves not being close together, the fluid being put into them leaks through the chinks and crevices. Superficial hearers lose the benefit of the word preached as the unseasoned vessel does the fluid; nor can any one hear to the saving of his soul unless he give most earnest heed."
—*Adam Clarke.*

"The best ground, untilled and neglected, soonest runs out into rank weeds. A man of knowledge that is either negligent or uncorrected can not but grow wild and godless."—*Bishop Hall*.

THE first word of the text arrests our attention. It indicates that what follows is necessarily based on what goes before. The author has stated an argument and reached a conclusion. He now declares an obligation and fortifies it with additional, proof. The gist of the argument runs thus: God, who revealed His truth through blundering men at sundry times and in divers manners until the world caught the inspiration and worshiped Him, has at last spoken through His own Son a clear message of unmistakable value. Therefore we ought to give most earnest heed. For if the word of angels and prophets was so confirmed by divine authority that no transgressor escaped the penalty of his offense under such preaching, how shall we escape if we neglect the gospel of the Son of God?

There have always been persons who could not understand the force of "divers manners;" people of such contracted powers as to render them utterly incapable of recognizing the gospel in its varied phases or when it appears in any other than the one form in which they have come to know it. They seem to forget that God has from the beginning been under the necessity of unfolding His truth in "divers manners" because of the diverse conditions among those to whom the revelation is made; that the real inspiration of the gospel records is found not in similarities, but in dissimilarities; that the evangelists, while reporting the same life, did not do it phonographically.

On the assumption that one knows truth when he sees it or hears it, and that he gives it a respectful consideration, the question is not how he receives it, but how he keeps it; whether the mind holds the truth it hears, or whether the heart is like the leaky barrel that lets that which is poured into it out through the cracks. It is one thing to receive truth and another thing to retain it. What one gets out of a religious service and keeps depends upon what kind of a heart-receptacle he brings to it. He who lets the truth slip has no adequate conception of the original Spokesman, the importance of His message, and the absolute necessity of the salvation of his own soul.

The only way to keep from letting the truth slip is to give earnest heed and to *hold* it in the mind. Neglect is all that is necessary to allow the truth to slip. It is a great thing to be a good listener and to read understandingly, but the value of the message received depends upon whether one apply it to himself or some one else. The real value of the sermon lies not in its possession as knowledge, but in its practice as deeds. Loss of ability is often synonymous with being out of practice. It is an easy thing to let the truth slip if you do not watch. Watch!

A TREE PLANTED BY THE RIVERS OF WATERS

"He shall be like a tree planted by the rivers of waters."—*Psalm i, 3.*

"The righteous shall flourish like the palm-tree; he shall grow like a cedar in Lebanon."—*Psalm xcii, 12.*

"Blessed is the man that trusteth in the Lord and whose hope the Lord is. For he shall be as a tree planted by the waters, and that spreadeth out his roots by the river, and shall not fear when heat cometh, but his leaf shall be green; and shall not be careful in the year of drought, neither shall cease from yielding fruit."—*Jeremiah xvii, 7, 8.*

> "How goodly are thy tents, O Jacob,
> Thy tabernacles, O Israel!
> As valleys are they spread forth,
> As gardens by the river-side,
> As lign-aloes which the Lord bath planted,
> As cedar trees beside the waters."
> —*Numbers xxiv, 5, 6.*

IT is interesting to note the numerous similes by which the Bible characterizes the righteous man. He is likened to the sun, the stars, the light; to gold, jewels, treasure, and precious stones; to lilies and pomegranates; to lions, eagles, sheep, and doves; to mountains and never-failing springs; to vines and trees and wheat and corn and salt. He is compared with everything representing strength and beauty, utility and loveliness. He is God's man and is in position to command the infinite resources of Almightiness.

In the first Psalm the righteous man is declared "blessed" and is likened to a "tree planted by the river." The characteristics which bring his blessedness are first described negatively. He must keep away from certain persons and their influence. The graces of the soul can not flourish when it is constantly subject to the contaminating power of sinful associations, but are rather liable to decay. The progression of the decadence is indicated by the words—walking, standing, sitting. Goodness must needs shun the very appearance of

Evil. To be on the safe side it is always well to heed the advice: "Enter not into the path of the wicked, and go not in the way of evil men. Avoid it, pass not by it, turn from it and pass away."

Negative virtue, however, is mainly valuable in proportion as it contributes to the positive. The wall around a garden serves a good purpose when it protects the growths within it. It is a good thing simply to abandon the seat of the scornful, but better to be filled with the spirit of God. The spirit-filled life hungers after righteousness; it delights in the law of the Lord. The trend of one's nature is always shown by the direction of his "delights." He who studies God's word to learn God's will, that he may do it, finds himself strong to resist temptation.

There are three words in the text which instantly engage the attention—tree, planted, and water. The tree has always been an eloquent figure to Orientals. The Fall of Eden had to do with the fruit of a tree, and the Vision of Redemption was that of a tree with healing leaves. The Psalmist has added to the image of a tree, the thought of "planted." His tree is no vagrant; its habitat is selected. It is in touch with water, the one requisite to turn a desert into a garden. Water is the symbol of life. To liken a man to "*a tree, planted by rivers of water*," is to compliment him highly.

The good man's life is "blessed" because it is deeply anchored in the Word of God. He is not exempt from wind and storm, but he has the power to outride them. Great fir trees that look like kings of the woodland are easily upset by the snarling storm because their roots run laterally in the surface gravel, while many a little sapling striking its roots deep down in earth meets the gale and stands unharmed. The prevailing fault of the religious life is shallowness. The consuming passion of commercial greed drives men so fast that they do not take time to be holy or even to meditate on God's holy law. There is a refreshing stream beneath the blistering sand of every vale of Baca, and he who will go far enough beneath the surface will never fail to find it.

The good man's life is fed by hidden springs. His soul drinks from the deep and ever-flowing rivers of God's abounding grace He has meat to eat that the world knows nothing of. The Church, with all for which it stands, is a perpetual fountain of all-enriching worth. Happy the man, the tendrils of whose soul drink from its limpid stream of life! He has depth and soundness and fructifying power because his roots run through the dust of superficial, fleeting things into the ever-flowing water. By what figure art thou characterized—a tree planted by the river, or chaff?

GOOD CONVERSATION

"Who is a wise man and endued with knowledge among you? Let him show out of a good conversation his works with meekness of wisdom."—*St. James iii, 13.*

"To him that ordereth his conversation aright will I show the salvation of God."—*Psalm i, 25.*

"A single conversation across the table with a wise man is worth a month's study of books."—*Chinese Proverb.*

"Those who have the true taste of conversation enjoy themselves in communicating each other's excellences, and not in triumphing over their imperfections."—*Addison.*

BENJAMIN FRANKLIN is the author of the statement, "Conversation warms the mind, enlivens the imagination, and is continually starting fresh game that is immediately pursued and taken, which would never have occurred in the duller intercourse of epistolary correspondence," and the Chinaman, judging from the proverb quoted above, seems to have learned that it is good to rub one's brain against another's, provided that other's be wise. Conversation opens the door of the soul and lets the inner man out and outer men in; it discovers common ground; it reveals hidden secrets and truths; it is a marvelous privilege and a fearful responsibility.

The greatest teachers and the most eminent expounders of law, philosophy, and religion have always been noted for their conversations. The student of comparative religion finds that the founders of the great faiths which have commanded the attention of the peoples of the world were colloquial in their best estates. The recorded colloquies of Zoroaster, Buddha, and Confucius constitute almost wholly the sacred writings of the religions they founded. The classical scholar is familiar with the dialogues of Plato, the face-to-face discussions of Socrates, the sayings of Aristotle, and the discourses of the peripatetic philosophers who taught their truths as they walked and talked with their pupils along the streets of Athens and the highways of

Greece. Christ was a great conversationalist, and His biographers record over one hundred interviews between Him and "kings, priests, judges, friends, foes, scoffers, inquirers, God, angels, and devils."

One does not converse long with others without telling them more than he thinks he has and without getting more from them than they are aware. Be careful! You may wake some day to see your blunders incarnate in another soul. There is no need of defining the term; everybody knows what is meant by good conversation. Unless one's conscience is miserably depraved it will tell him when his conversation is good and when the inter-communication is bad.

Good conversation is the index of a clean heart. "If any man offend not in word, the same is a perfect man." As the jingle of a coin reveals its soundness or exposes it as a counterfeit, so man is known by his spoken words. Speech, like children, will not deceive, and is constantly "telling tales" about the personality from which it comes. A woman who called at her neighbor's door was met by the little girl, who, as she opened the door, said, "Mamma is n't at home." "Why, I saw her through the window," said the visitor. "Yes," said the little girl, "but she saw you first." Words sometimes unwittingly expose a lying heart. When the waters of the stream are sweet, no one will suspect that the fountain-head is bitter; and if the waters are bitter no one will believe that the fountain can be sweet.

Good conversation is always based upon "the truth, the whole truth, and nothing but the truth," and never forgets to season its justice with most generous mercy. It scorns tale-bearing and considers evil communication contemptible. It regards the gossip as an ill-mannered wretch, with a mouth like the opening of a sewer system which empties its foul contents into some clear lake and pollutes the waters for miles around. In the presence of good conversation, slang and threadbare puns, and crude and silly utterances, and the dirty story with its vile suggestiveness, slink away as lizards and vermin, and creeping, slimy creatures into holes and darkness because they can not bear the light.

Good conversation always has God as a silent third party, and often as the speaking and listening second. Man may walk and talk with his Maker.

> "With Him sweet converse I maintain;
> Great as He is I dare be free;

> I tell Him all my grief and pain,
>   And He reveals His love to me."

A little conversation with the Master sets everything all right. What a blessed thought that God will listen to man's stammering prattle; yea, that He will stop making a world to bend His ear to catch a weak child's whisper!

> "I saw a little child with bandaged eyes,
>   Put up its hand to feel its mother's face;
> She bent and took the tender, groping palms,
>   And pressed them to her lips, a little space.
>
> "I know a soul made blind by its desires,
>   And yet its faith keeps feeling for God's face—
> Bend down, O mighty love, and let that faith
>   One little moment, touch thy lips of Grace."

THE DAY'S WORK

"I must work the works of Him that sent Me while it is day; the night cometh, when no man can work."—*John ix, 4.*

"The taskmasters were urgent, saying, Fulfill your works, your daily tasks." (Marginal reading, "a matter of a day in his day.")—*Exodus v, 13.*

"A Christian's spirituality will depend as much upon his work as his work upon his spirituality."—*Chalmers.*

> "O blessed work for Jesus!
> O rest at Jesus' feet!
> There toil seems pleasure,
> My wants are treasure,
> And pain for Him is sweet.
> Lord, if I may,
> I'll serve another day."
> —*Anna B. Warner.*

"Neither is this a work of one day or two."—*Ezra x. 13.*

WHEN Jesus and His disciples came across the man who was born blind, the question (so perplexing to all thoughtful minds), What regulates the distribution of suffering? arose. Is the rod of suffering a rod of chastisement? If so, what is the cause of the fault that makes the correction necessary? Is one's affliction necessarily the result of his own sin, or of the sin of his parents, or of the sin of anybody? No one knows, except in instances where science is able to determine the inevitable consequences of the breaking of Nature's laws. With the simple sweep of a telling sentence the Lord impresses His hearers with the truth that the all-important question is not how the man got into the difficulty, but how he can be helped out. The latter may involve the former, but let it ever be remembered that it is one thing to pry into the cause of suffering for the mere purpose of locating the blame or of exonerating one's self from the claims of pity and charity, and it is a wholly different thing to inquire into the cause so as more effectually to deal with the effect. No matter how sin and suffering came, the fact is that they are here. Their presence creates an opportunity to work for God. To rid the world of evil, of wretchedness, of lonely sorrow, of destitution, and disease, is man's plain duty. Man, would you work for God, be in your own little way eyes to the blind, feet to the lame, and help to the helpless.

He who has any real regard for "the day's work" recognizes a purpose in his life and sees opportunities as "he passes by;" he believes that it is worth while to stop to help a person here and there. Jesus practically said to His disciples: "I am here as a representative of My Father, who sent Me, and in the fleeting moments of My earthly pilgrimage I must not lose an opportunity to fulfill My mission, which is to preach good tidings to the meek, to bind up the broken-hearted, to proclaim liberty to the captive, to restore sight to the blind, to proclaim the acceptable year and also the day of vengeance of the Almighty, to comfort them that mourn, to give beauty for ashes, and the garment of praise for the spirit of heaviness."

Every soul is sent into the world with a task. Man is God's representative, and his capital is a trust. He is not a designer, his business is to build according to pattern. His errand is commensurate with his capability. His personal responsibility is based upon his endowment, but his endowment is expansive, and he is responsible for the expanding of it. Every man has his day. Each day has its task. The day's work must be done in the daytime. Wasted opportunities can never be redeemed, especially after the sun has set. One has well said, "There are four things that come not back; the spoken word, the sped arrow, the past life, and the neglected opportunity." Life is limited, and its days speed ever faster to the end. Work while the day lasts. No one can work by night who has failed to work by day.

THE HEART'S INCLINATION

"Incline your heart unto the Lord God."—*Joshua xxiv, 23*.

"Almost every one has a predominant inclination to which his other desires and affections submit, and which governs him, though perhaps with some intervals, through the whole course of his life."—*Hume*.

"Trust in the Lord with all thy heart; and lean not unto thine own understanding."—*Proverbs iii, 5*.

"God never accepts a good inclination instead of a good action, where that action may be done; nay, so much the contrary, that, if a good inclination be not seconded by a good action, the want of that action is made so much the more criminal and inexcusable."—*South*.

"I have inclined my heart to perform Thy statutes."—*Psalm cxix, 112*.

By some strange law persons and things discover their affinities. If it were not for the blunders of some men and women, the rule would be universally true. Vegetation loves the light and puts itself out to show its affection. It will lean toward the grimy window through which only the faintest ray can come; pull itself around a corner if only it can catch a glimpse of morning, and says, "If I can not have light, let me pine away and die." Positive electricity will leap toward its negative counterpart and strike hands in happy greeting and inseparable union. The magnetic needle may be dragged out of its peaceful associations, but it knows its place and will never cease tugging until it gets back again. When the sun looks up over the eastern rim of day, its face all ruddy with the blush of morning and shining with the radiance of a warm-hearted smile, every fairy of the springtime comes out to meet him in gay attire. God never meant that any bird should fail to find its mate or that any soul should lose its way and fail to enter heaven. O, pity the folly of men's blundering hearts! Man was made to live with God, and can not live without Him. The child, true compass of the celestial realm pointing ever toward the heavenly Polaris, represents the heart's right inclination. To men bent with sin and bound with its curse, the Master said, "Except ye be converted and become as little children, ye can not find the way to heaven."

Every person has a bent. Every heart leans toward some attraction. Every soul craves somewhat. Every nature prays to some god. Every life feels the need of some kind of companionship. Every individual seeks the fellowship of some other, either better or worse. Some are positive in their decisions, and some have gone no farther than to *lean* in certain directions for certain more or less well-defined reasons. With reference to a godly life, the last named are in a sort of semi-neutral, disinterested, passive state—not wholly disinclined, yet not particularly inclined. They make religion synonymous with denominationalism, and while they never have identified themselves with any organization, they "lean" toward the Methodist Episcopal, Presbyterian, Baptist, or some other, as the case may be. Man, woman, halting soul, God does not care toward what creed you lean He wants you to incline your heart toward Him!

The heart's inclination indicates its tastes. What variety in the likes and dislikes of men! There are those who seem to relish the coarse and degraded, while others delight in the beautiful and good. Taste is a subjective faculty, and may be cultivated and refined, or debased and jaded. The appreciation of the classical in art, literature, and music is acquired, and the evil habits which mark the decadence of a soul are a matter of schooling. One's tastes and the whole trend of his life may be changed by both education and dissipation. A real desire to change for the better is Repentance; the change itself is what we call Conversion.

The heart's inclination is controlled by its choices. He who really chooses draws a sharp and well-defined line between what he accepts and what he rejects. When the alternatives are good and evil, right and wrong, godliness and sinfulness, and the line is definitely drawn, you have what is called *"a clear conversion."* A genuine conversion is simply the absolute rejection of all evil and the positive acceptance of all good, with the divine smile of approval on the act. Resolutions are good if they mark well determined limits and are kept for conscience's sake. Whether one is inclined *to* or *from* the right depends upon what his will has chosen. Conversion is turning with God's help to the north-star course and forsaking all other ways.

God inclines toward the heart that inclines toward Him, but the soul's attitude must be hearty, and not simply formal, or it will not command His attention. The mere mumbling of the formulae of worship and the reciting of ritualistic rites are intolerably repulsive to a Being who desires rather the spiritual fellowship of His children. The Heavenly Father is most wonderfully kind and will come a long distance to meet a sick heart that leans toward Him. A pale, puny little plant leaned toward the window to see the light, and the good Sun said, as it caressed the drooping, sickly leaves, "I came ninety-three million miles to cheer your heart." And the little plant blushed a little deeper green and felt better. God is just like the sun. Soul, you will never find your real affinity until you lean toward Him. Incline your heart toward God, and Heavenly Grace will run to meet you.

PUFFED UP AND BUILT UP

"Knowledge puffeth up, but love buildeth up." —*1 Corinthians viii, 1.*

"Conceit may puff a man up, but never can prop him up."—*Ruskin.*

"If its colors were but fast colors, self-conceit would be a most comfortable quality. Bat life is so humbling, mortifying, disappointing to vanity, that the great man's idea of himself gets washed out of him by the time he is forty."—*C. Buxton.*

"The brightest blaze of intelligence is of incalculably less value than the smallest spark of charity."—*W. Nevins.*

"It is possible that a man should be so changed by love as hardly to be recognized as the same person."—*Terence.*

THE subject of this text has both a general and a particular significance. In general, head-power dissociated from heart-power is cold and unsympathetic, selfish and exclusive and uncharitable. In particular the text is related to the question of religious liberty based upon a boasted enlightenment on the one hand, and a generous love that takes into consideration the weakness and foibles of brother-man on the other.

Paul addressed these words to a society partly heathen and partly Christian. Many questions concerning religious principle and practice would naturally arise in such a community as this. The statement with reference to knowledge and love is part of the answer to a letter which the apostle had received from the liberal and self-conceited party who had come to scorn those who had scruples. The scrupulous, however, deemed the liberals less godly and consistent than themselves.

A condition of self-satisfied enlightenment and supposed self-righteousness which erects a barrier between itself and imagined or real weakness, is a dangerous and destructive situation. One stands on slippery places who only possesses a knowledge which puffs him up with self-esteem. Wealth, social or educational ad vantages, position, imagined physical beauty, or inherited reputation or blue blood, or other stuff for which they were never obliged to work, sometimes exalt people with ideas of superior self-importance; but it does n't take much of a puncture to flatten such persons out. There are, however, certain other qualities which, if builded into people, make them solid from the ground up and firm with the enduring qualities of eternal love: the world's battering rams can not beat down such a citadel as that.

The knowledge that puffeth up is ever the "little learning," which "is a dangerous thing." The more deeply men drink at the fountain of wisdom, the more is their knowledge tempered with humility. Greatness and goodness in the last analysis are the same. God is good and "God is love," and man is therefore both wisest and best when most filled with the divinest love. The great question underlying all service is not so much one of intellect as one of heart. Human life needs not so much more information as passionate, clinging, constant, self-sacrificing love. Love will build up manhood and will furnish the only solid foundation for all political, social, and so-called secular affairs.

The ideal possession is neither knowledge without love nor love without knowledge; not more of the one and less of the other, but more of both. Combined in most ample measure, they form the impregnable fortress of God in man. It is only when men know the most and love the best that they most fully understand the true meaning of liberty. To know God is to love Him, and to love Him is to be charitable with all His children.

The Christian life is a beautiful and symmetrical unity. It combines the head and the heart. It is something solid, firm, substantial, which has been builded out of indestructible material. It is a life governed by principle. It carefully distinguishes between the essential and the non-essential. It is conscientious. It regards the rights of others while demanding its own. It both knows and feels. It has enduring elements. It is not puffed up, it is built up. It has knowledge, and at the same time love. Are you a Christian?

ANGELS' FOOD

"Man did eat angels' food."—*Psalm lxxxviii, 25*.

"A fig for your bill of fare; show me your bill of company."—*Swift*.

"The features come insensibly to be formed and to assume their shape from the frequent and habitual expression of certain affections of the soul. These affections are marked on the countenance; nothing is more certain than this; and when they turn into habits, they must leave on it durable impressions."—*Rousseau*.

"Your fathers did eat manna in the wilderness and they died. . . . I am the bread of life. . . . If any man shall eat of this bread he shall live forever."—*St. John vi, 48, 49, 51*.

A MORE literal translation of the text would probably be, "Man did eat the dainty morsels of the princes, or mighty ones." The reference, of course, is to the manna that fell in the wilderness, but there is a certain subtle suggestiveness in the statement which makes us cry out with hunger of heart and with an understanding we can not express in words, "Lord, evermore give us this bread!" No one who has ever tasted the sweet food of heaven will ever again be satisfied with the coarse pabulum of the world. He had been nourished on these spiritual riches who said, "O, taste and see that the Lord is good!"

The great storehouse of God is filled with all sorts of nourishment for all conditions of men—milk for babes, strong meat for toiling man, and angels' corn for those who can assimilate celestial food. He who goes hungry, sins against the abundance of his Father's house. Many men go hungry because they have no taste for what is good, and others have no power to appropriate its worth. One may eat out of the dish with the Savior, and if he have the heart of a Judas he might as well feed upon the coarse fodder of the devil's husks. He who dines upon the Bread of Life and assimilates it will find himself changed into the likeness of Christ from glory to glory.

He who satisfies his heart-hunger with the bounties of God's banqueting-table feasts on heavenly manna and knows the taste of angel's food. When the things of earth no longer have the power to still the cravings of the soul, look up by faith and find thy famine relieved by the amplitude of the plenteousness of God's good things. Hungry soul, and faint, the table is ready; you may feed upon the delicacies prepared for the princes of the Father's house!

A careful diet is one of the first prerequisites to health. One's condition, physical, mental, moral, depends largely upon the food with which he nourishes these respective phases of his being. It is strange but true that men will knowingly feed upon the things which harm them. It is easy to tell by one's manner and appearance, in whatever realm of life's activities you may meet him, in what fields he finds his pasture. He who eats angel's food will grow angel-like. There are all too many who, recognizing this truth, are trying to become angelic by feeding on stale manna, having forgotten that it must needs be gathered fresh every morning.

The ancients talked about ambrosia, the immortality-giving food of the gods. Here is a statement in the Book of Truth to the effect that men have eaten Bread of Heaven. The Mightiest of all the sons of men came, saying: "I am the Bread of Life. If any man eat of this bread he shall live forever." Blessed fact! Men may still eat angel's food! "Feed on it by faith, and may it preserve thee soul and body unto everlasting life."

CROOKED WAYS

"Such as turn aside unto their crooked ways."—*Psalm cxxv, 5.*

"Ye may be blameless and harmless, the sons of God, without rebuke in the midst of a crooked and perverse nation, among whom ye shine as lights."—*Philippians ii, 15.*

"Their feet run to evil . . . there is no judgment in their goings; they have made them crooked paths."—*Isaiah lix, 8.*

"I will go before thee and make the crooked places straight."
—*Isaiah xiv, 2.*

"Every valley shall be exalted, and every mountain and hill shall be made low; and the crooked shall be made straight, and the rough places plain; and the glory of the Lord shall be revealed."—*Isaiah xl, 4.*

YOU can't do much with a crooked stick. My father once built a barn, in the days when it was thought that the frame-work of such a structure had to be made of hewn timbers. We went out into the woods and hunted for tall, straight trees and saplings out of which to make the beams, plates, posts, sleepers, and girders. Some of the beams had to be eight inches square and forty feet in length—a crooked stick could not be used. We backwoods-men know that the best stave-bolts, railroad-ties, and fence-rails are made from straight, clean stuff. About all that can be done with a crooked stick is to cut it into fire-wood, and even then it is hard to split. Crooked timber is not of much account.

There are men sometimes who are called "poor sticks," which is equivalent to calling them "crooked," for a crooked stick is poor. A crooked man, however, is worth less than a crooked stick in proportion as a straight man is worth more than *any* stick. It is bad enough to be a stick—some men are; but worse to be a crooked one. A man's crookedness manifests itself in his conduct. O, what a pity that business, politics, society, and religion have to be damaged by the crooked ways of unscrupulous men and women!

There are different names for the life quality manifest in those who turn aside from the straight road into the bewildering mazes of crooked paths. In the commercial world it is called dishonesty; in the political, sycophancy; in the social, rascality; and in the religious, hypocrisy. He who walks in crooked roads is the owner either of a restless conscience or a dead one; he dissipates his strength in by-paths and increases the distance between the beginning and the end of any worthy achievement in life.

The first proposition that the student of Euclid is called upon to demonstrate is that a straight line is the shortest distance between two points. This statement is true in the realm of the unseen as well as the seen. In a world where there are either real or figurative mountains to be climbed or tunneled, rivers to be bridged or forded, chasms to be crossed or avoided, desert stretches without an oasis sprawling across the journey, it is not always an easy thing to travel from one point to another in a bee-line; but he who would take the straightest road, and therefore the shortest, must recognize that right or left from the air-line, even by the breadth of a hair, is off the track.

There is a difference between the person who tries to walk straightly, but wabbles on account of weakness, and the one who deliberately turns aside into crooked ways. Man's worst sin is not weakness, but wilfulness. The will is the seat both of the soul's authority and its responsibility. The course of one's life lies in the direction of his choice. Where there is a will there is a way, and where there is a right will there is a straight way. The very heart of God is hurt when man chooses to turn aside into crooked ways.

The road that leads to enduring life is straight, and no one who walks crookedly can keep on the highway which is not only straight but narrow. He who spends too much time in crooked ways and by-roads will not have time to cover the space between earth and heaven, and even if he could manage to reach the gate in time, he can not enter with empty hands. On either side of the beaten path to glory there are perils of beasts and robbers, and the liability of becoming lost in a trackless waste filled with pit-falls and delusive snares.

The quickest and surest way to the goal of life is direct. It is a highway; to turn aside is to go down hill. He who gets off the track finds it hard to get on again, for the slopes are steep. Blessed promise! The Guide will go before, to make the way straight! Follow the Guide. Keep straight. It takes a single eye, a level head, and a true heart to walk straightly. You can keep on the straight road if you will.

THE SIGNS OF AN APOSTLE

"I seek not yours, but you. . . . And I will most gladly spend and be spent for you."—*2 Corinthians xii, 14, 15.*

> "The proud he tamed, the penitent he cheered;
> Nor to rebuke the rich offender, feared;
> His preaching much, but more his practice wrought,
> A living sermon of the truth he taught."—*Dryden.*

"The minister is to be a real man, a live man, a true man, a simple man; great in his love, in his life, in his work, in his simplicity, in his gentleness."—*John Hall.*

"Men of God have always from time to time walked among men, and made their commission felt in the heart and soul of the commonest hearer."—*Emerson.*

"For I determined not to know anything among you, save Jesus Christ, and Him crucified."—*1 Corinthians ii, 2.*

IT was difficult for some of the Corinthians to believe that Paul was really an apostle. They had such queer ideas of the characteristics which they supposed belonged to the man who was sent from God. A preacher is a very uncanny creature in the eyes of some folks. They keep him at a safe distance and associate his life with the most mysterious unreality. They would agree with the gentleman who is reputed to have said, "There are three genders in the human race—men, women, and preachers." This ridiculous conception arises partly from the foolishness and ignorance of benighted souls who mistake their own superstition for religious faith, and partly from the long hair, sable garments, and somber countenances of would-be pretenders in the preacher-cult. I hereby make my humble confession that I have seen priestly personages so fearfully and wonderfully clad that I would as lief have had their friendship as that of Hamlet's ghost. If one of these were seen in public the world would be justified in running away from "it." But Paul was none of these, and his apostolicity was only assailed because the contracted littleness of his critics could not comprehend the suggestiveness and blessedness of his free, genial, and generous intercourse among his fellow-men. God pity the perspective in which some men view the cross!

It is a shock to some people to learn that ministers do not have incipient wings. That is hard, but in reality it is no worse than for a minister to find out that some of the official-saints, pew-holders, Sunday-school teachers, and church-workers of various sorts need a few finishing touches before they are quite ready to be translated. The fact is that God made all His children out of clay, "and He gave some to be apostles, and some prophets, and some evangelists, and some teachers, and some pastors," and we are all in the work of "going on to perfection" and of helping others on. The fight is both within and without, and many a time the minister, as well as the private saint, is obliged to arise and restrain himself by force, and literally beat his meanness into subjection, and by the grace of God to climb out of the pit, lest when he has preached to others he himself should be a castaway.

What, then, are the earmarks of an apostle? Is there any unmistakable sign of dress or mien? Is a man an apostle because he wears a long black coat and face? Is it an indication that one has received divine orders if he manifest a commercial imbecility and an ignorance of the business world? Is a fellow with a Bible under his arm sure to be sent from God? Is the formalism of a religious functionary necessarily a badge of apostleship? The answer to such questions must ever be, "Maybe yes, and maybe no." There are, however, some tests which never fail.

The first sign of an apostle in pulpit or pew, and the mark by which he is always known, is consecrated manliness. Godliness that makes a man unnatural (if we dare think of such a thing) can never exert much influence over natural men. Nothing is more Christlike than a sanely virtuous man. A lot of so-called religion is *insanity*. "Vir" was the Latin word for man, and it is the root of the English "virtue." One must be manly before he can be saintly.

No man can claim to be an apostle whose record is not backed up, certified, and glorified by hard work. The God-sent man has a stupendous task. Some people think an apostle has a snap. Foolish error! The true prophet burns out his very life in fiery zeal. Lazy souls there are, but the time-server is never heaven sent, whether he be a preacher, a hod-carrier, or a seer. The true badge of apostleship is the spirit that seeks not to be ministered unto, but to minister—that is willing to spend and to be spent for others. The true apostle seeks not to satisfy a vaulting ambition, but to serve; his business is related to what men are, and not what they have. If he stand in the pulpit, clothed with divine authority, he must always be able to say, "I seek not yours, but you."

SELF-MASTERY

"He that bath no rule over his own spirit is like a city that is broken down and without walls."—*Proverbs xxv, 28.*

"He who reigns within himself and rules his passions, desires, and fears, is more than a king."—*Milton.*

"Do you want to know the man against whom you have most reason to guard yourself? Your looking-glass will give you a very fair likeness of his face."—*Whately.*

"If you would learn self-mastery, begin by yielding yourself to the One Great Master."—*Lobstein.*

"True dignity abides with him alone who, in the silent hour of inward thought, can still suspect and still revere him-self in lowliness of heart."—*Wordsworth.*

"No man is free who can not command himself."—*Pythagoras.*

"He that is slow to anger is better than the mighty; and he that miens his spirit than he that taketh a city."—*Proverbs xvi, 32.*

THE text is a striking simile. It suggests that the man who controls his own powers creates his own defense, but that the one who lets the forces of his being run riot has no bulwark for his life. Its picture tells the tale of two cities—one, walled, garrisoned, fortified, with citadel strong and impregnable. The enemy's battering rams only beat themselves into splinters in a vain attempt to force a breach; the missiles and javelins, though hurled with might, fall short and do not reach the top; the citizens, protected by a strong defense, sit secure and dwell in peace and safety; the other, defenseless, with broken walls, and unprotected tower—a prey to plunderers and an invitation to hostile hordes. The dwellers lie among the ruins or hide in wretched huts, an easy mark for flying darts, and, unprotected, they quake with fear.

Man's battle royal is with himself. The most dangerous powers which threaten his destruction are not outside, but inside his life. His strength is measured by the power of the feelings he subdues, and not by the power of those which subdue him. It takes more strength to forgive an injury than to pay back its evil in double measure. He who loses control of his temper is controlled by it, and, therefore, a slave. "Keep cool," says Webster; "anger is not argument." It is said that Socrates used to check his anger by talking low. The record of his dealings with his wife, Xantippe, shows him to be a man who had acquired a remarkable self-control. It is a great thing to have brains, but it is a greater thing to command them.

The command, "Work out your own salvation," is only another way of saying, "Master yourself." He who undertakes to conquer his own spirit has a long warfare and a hard fight. Ask the man who has contended with principalities and powers within his heart, who has wrestled with the beast of appetite and fought with giants of habit, what he knows about the battle and how fierce the struggle is. Even after the enemy has been brought under the yoke the guard must be kept on duty. Reformation must be continuous or it will never be complete. Seneca says, "We should ask ourselves every night: What infirmity have I mastered to-day? What temptation resisted? What virtue acquired?"

One is your Master, and you have only mastered self as His spirit has mastered you. He conquers by love. Some one has illustrated the truth by the following dialogue: "I'll master it," said the ax, and its blows fell heavy on the iron; but each blow only made its edge more dull, until it ceased to strike. "Leave it to me," said the saw, and with its relentless teeth it worked backwards and forwards till they were all worn off. "Ha! Ha!" said the hammer; "I'll show you the way;" but at his first fierce stroke his head flew off, and the iron remained as before. "Shall I try?" asked the small, soft flame. It curled gently around the iron and embraced it and never left it until it melted under the resistless influence. So love subdues a heart. Christ is love incarnate. When He rules, love rules. He is the great Teacher. Learn of Him. Xenophon tells how the Persian princes had for their teachers the four best men in the kingdom— the wisest, to teach wisdom; the bravest, to teach courage; the most just, to teach morality; and the most temperate, to teach self-control. The Christian finds all these in the man Christ Jesus.

God will not defend the citadel of any man's life until the man himself has built up the breach in front of his own door. Hast thou conquered self? There is really no other battle to be fought. Take the advice of Napoleon to his brother Joseph, of Spain "I have only one counsel for you—'Be master.'" But, Soul, for thee, Let that mastery be a mastery over self.

THE SCHOOL OF EXPERIENCE

"I have learned by experience."—*Genesis xxx, 27*.

"Experience is the Lord's school, and they who are taught by Him usually learn by the mistakes they make that in themselves they have no wisdom; and by their slips and falls that they have no strength."
—*John Newton*.

"When I was young I was sure of everything; in a few years, having been mistaken a thousand times, I was not half so sure of most things as I was before; at present, I am hardly sure of anything but what God has revealed to me."—*John Wesley*.

"Experience keeps a dear school; but fools will learn in no other, and scarce in that; for it is true that we may give advice, but we can not give conduct."—*Benjamin Franklin*.

"Experience takes dreadfully high school-wages; but he teaches like no other."—*Carlyle*.

"I have learned . . . I am instructed."—*Paul*.

EVERY young person passes through a state when he sets no value on experience; when hope is a bigger word than history; when he wants no advice from his elders, because he thinks he needs none. Talk to him about what you've learned by experience, and he will tell you to attend to your own affairs. As to the matter of what is best for him, he can not be instructed—he knows it all. It is well, perhaps, that the stripling gets a momentary satisfaction out of his imagined wisdom, for he never in all his after life feels so wise again. It is possible to be in the school of experience and hardly know it until the first real test comes. With reference to the individual, the first actual achievement in knowledge has been made when he can say, "I have learned by experience."

There is a sense in which one ought to forget the things which are behind and reach out after things before. Lot's wife was turned into a pillar of salt because she even looked back toward the smoking city of sin. Jesus once said,

"He who putteth his hand to the plow and looketh backward is not fit for the kingdom of God." But, in these instances, the rebuke is for the proneness to cherish and foster the mistakes by-gone, and not for the spirit that would seek to profit by them. A very wise man is reputed to have said, "The prudent man foreseeth the evil and hideth himself;" but it is fair to admit that his prudence is more often a result of experience than a gift of prophetic insight. Other things being equal, when a thoughtful man says, "I have learned," it is time to stop and listen.

When I emphasize the value of experience I do not wish to be understood to say that mere age will bring discretion. It is a common remark that an old fool is the worst kind of a fool. Young people are sometimes found whose wisdom far excels the wisdom of their elders. The business world recognizes the fact that youth may be sharp-eyed, level-headed, and judicious. What I am trying to say is, that, given any individual, bright or dull, with whatsoever powers inherent or acquired, and his wisdom will be enlarged, his soundness increased, and his capability magnified when he reaches the vantage-ground of experience and can say, "I have learned."

The school of experience is the oldest university in the world—it was founded in the Garden of Eden. Since the foundation of the institution God has been its leading teacher, and His instruction is accurate. The value of any school depends largely on the capability of its faculty. What a handicap to be obliged to unlearn what incompetent instructors have taught us! On the other hand, the virtue of the very best instruction is conditioned on how the student appropriates its worth.

The school of experience is the largest college in the world, having as many students as there are persons in the human race. Its catalogue shows every grade of personality lying between the most superstitious savagery and the most fastidious refinement. The discipline and instruction of such an immense aggregation of diverse elements is a stupendous task, and God has the right to expect the help of many tutors. God's truant laws are strict. Every soul must pass through the school, but all do not profit alike by its instructions.

The school of experience is an expensive institution, and its curriculum is very hard. It costs a lot of money to take the course, and often a lot of time. One may or may not know books, but before he can get a diploma from this university he *must* have good sense. The parchment of the school is a refined heart, and its seal bears the image of the Great Teacher. It is impossible to pass through life and not be enrolled in the school of experience. The institution will do one of two things for you: It will harden and embitter, or it will soften and sweeten your heart. You yourself determine which. If you do not allow God to be your teacher, or if you misinterpret His discipline, your experience will drag you down: but if you allow Omniscience to be your master, and believe that whom the Lord loveth. He sometimes permits to be chastened, you will find yourself enriched, ennobled, refined, and rendered more worthy of heaven.

A BLEMISHED OFFERING

"But whatsoever bath a blemish, that shall ye not offer; for it shall not be acceptable for you."—*Leviticus xxii, 20.*

"Christ loved the Church and gave Himself for it, . . . that He might present it unto Himself a glorious Church not having spot or wrinkle, or any such thing; but that it should be holy and without blemish."—*Ephesians v, 26, 27.*

> "O, for a lowly contrite heart,
> Believing, true, and clean,
> Which neither life nor death can part
> From Him that dwells within.
>
> A heart in every thought renewed,
> And full of love divine;
> Perfect, and right, and pure, and good,
> A copy, Lord, of Thine."—*Charles Wesley.*

> "Not what we give, but what we share
> For the gift without the giver is bare."
> —*Vision of Sir Lowell*

THE original idea of *offering* was something brought near to the altar or to God, and did not express so much the neutral idea of a gift as it denoted a complimentary present made to secure and retain good-will. The fundamental idea was to gratify God by giving Him, or sharing with Him, a meal. Eating and drinking together were the ordinary symbols of friendship. A bond between man and God was supposedly created by this interchange of hospitality. The idea was to entertain God at a feast in which He should receive His portion of the food in the fragrant, fire-distilled essence which arose in the savor of the burning meat. It was thought that the honor thus accorded to Him so gratified Him as to render Him well-disposed toward the worshipers.

The origin and development of the idea of sacrifice and offering down to the time when the worshiper came into possession of the thought that

"Obedience is better than sacrifice," affords a most interesting study and shows how crude have been the ideas and superstitions intertwined with the beginnings of the religious genius. There came a time when the prophets denounced sacrifice, according to the prescribed rites, as meaningless, and represented God as declining to countenance offerings, sated with them, and even loathing them. God's attitude is expressed in these words, "To what purpose is the multitude of your sacrifices to Me? I delight not in the blood of bullocks, or of lambs, or of he-goats. Bring no more vain oblations." The inference is that morality would count far more with Him.

It must be said, however, in justice to the ancient Israelites, that, notwithstanding their crude ideas of the proper method of approach to God, and of the acts which would be a delight to Him, they had reached such a refined sense of the fitness of things as to recognize the fact that nothing in the way of a gift but the very best and soundest was fit to offer to a perfect God. The fact that a law had to be enacted to regulate the matter would seem to indicate that some one had been picking out the blemished animals in his flock to offer in sacrifice.

Leaving out of the question the form of the offering and the method of giving it, it is true now, as ever, that nothing short of the best that one can offer will be acceptable to God. Too often man is inclined to keep the best and give the rest. He will give a stingy portion (and let go of it grudgingly) of the money that is left after every other interest has been considered, to support the enterprises of the Kingdom; he will patronize other things with his presence in sun, or rain, or frost, or darkness, and squeeze out a scanty interest in the services of the House of Prayer in the very finest weather; he prays when he is sick, when his heart is burdened, and when he is sleepy and tired out at the close of day. O, brother, this is wrong! It is an insult to God to bring before Him a blemished offering, unless a blemished offering is all one has.

The gift must be sanctified on the altar of the life of the giver. The offering is always blemished when the offerer is unsound. A blemished heart can not offer an unblemished sacrifice. He who would have his offering sound and unblemished must get right himself. The heart must be both new and clean. There is no such thing as patching up matters with hypocritical oblations. These are blemished offerings, and are not acceptable. The principle of the blemished offering is wrong, since it fails to put first things first. God and the interests of His kingdom are first. There must be no other gods before Him. To bring to the altar a second-class offering is to rob both self and God. It would be more honorable to be openly a rebellious infidel than to fail to give the best. Give Him your best.

THE PRICE OF A WORTHY WORK

"Jesus knew that virtue had gone out of Him."—*St. Mark v, 30*.

"The force, the mass of character, mind, heart, or soul that a man can put into any work, is the most important factor in that work."
—*A. P. Peabody*.

"Whatsoever thy hand findeth to do, do it with thy might."
—*Ecclesiastes ix, 10*.

"To color well requires your life. It can not be done cheaper."
—*Ruskin*.

"The good shepherd giveth His life for the sheep."—*St. John x, 11*.

"Labor—the expenditure of vital effort in some form—is the measure, nay, it is the maker of values."—*J. G. Holland*.

THE Son of man was a busy man. He said once, "My Father worketh hitherto, and I work." There is no record of any attempt on His part to get something for nothing. He never tried to get people to follow Him by holding out the inducement of an easy time. He spoke of bonds, and stripes, and crosses, and persecutions, and imprisonments, and afflictions, and virtually said, "He who is looking for an easy road to Glory should not try to follow Me." He never said, "Come unto Me all ye who are idle and looking for case," but His call was to those "who labor and are heavy laden." He did hard things, and said, "Follow Me." He was willing to spend His energy to the last ounce if by giving His life He could save His fellows. He literally poured out His soul as a healing lotion upon the bleeding wounds of earth. The power that proceeded from Him was the force of a heaven-born passion. He knew that to save His own life meant a mission unfulfilled. He, therefore, gave His life without stint—passionately gave it, that men might know the value of a truly generous heart. The healing virtue of His burning soul streamed forth and fell on halt, and lame, and blind, until scores of helpless leapt and walked and saw with joy. Multitudes thronged His presence, if only to come near enough to touch the hem of the garment of a man who was willing to share His life with others, and ever since He walked and talked and worked with men, myriads have taken up the cross, and, following after Him, have cried, "In hoc signo vinces."

There is no approach to the Elysian fields except by the way of the cross. Heaven is not reached by an easier way. An ancient Greek, thinking to save his bees a laborious flight to Hymettus, clipped their wings and gathered flowers for them to work upon at home, but they made no honey. Worthy work is always hard work, and only he who is willing to pay the price may enjoy the fruits of honest toil. "O, if I could put a dream like that on canvas!" exclaimed an enthusiastic young artist. "Dream on canvas!" growled the old master. "It is ten thousand touches which you must learn to put on canvas which makes your dream."

It costs something to do a thing right, but he who has any decent regard for his conscience dare not do it otherwise. He who likes his job takes it to bed with him, walks with it in the daytime, puts his heart, hands, brains, and life into it, and is bound to succeed; and, more than that, he who puts his soul into his work is always satisfied with results. Emerson says that the reward of a thing well done is to have done it. The heaven that lies at the end of any pilgrimage is reached by a path both rough and steep. Stupidity sits down on the way, gives up, and faints. No one was ever best in any station who did not buy his honor with his blood.

It is an easy step from doing poor work in a half-hearted way to doing wrong. There is a satirical poem which represents the devil out fishing for men, and adapting his bait to the tastes and temperaments of his prey. It shows that the lazy idler is the easiest victim, for he will swallow even the naked hook. He who is shiftless by choice will soon become nerveless and powerless by necessity. It is a law of nature that unused faculties become degenerate. "It is better to wear out than to rust out."

No person ever did anything worth while who was not conscious of the fact that virtue had gone out of him. The heart that truly serves is doomed to bleed. The life that heaven crowns at last must pay the full measure of devotion to its task. No one who prays, "Thy kingdom come," with an honest heart, dare lay down his work till the wounds of the world have all been healed. There is the *hireling* method, and there is the *good shepherd* method. Use either, as you choose, but be fully aware of the *consequences*! It is possible for one simply to exist and to consume his powers by rust and slow combustion, but he who really lives must blaze with a consuming passion and burn up his fuel in a furnace flame. The price of redemption is always blood, and blood means life.

MADE OVER

"And the vessel that he made of clay was marred in the hand of the potter; so he made it again."—*Jeremiah xviii, 4.*

"Away back in your life God took you and placed you upon the wheel, and for these many years has sought to make you fair. But there has come a flaw and break, and you are a piece of broken pottery. Your life is marred, your ideal broken, and all round you lie the littered pieces of the man or woman that you might have been. But now what shall you do? God put you in your place for a high purpose, but you have missed your mark. God might take another piece of clay and make that a vessel, but instead He comes again to seek you. The broken pieces of your life, your marred and spoiled ideal, may be made over again. The hand of God is, so to speak, laying hold upon the broken pieces of your marred and spoiled life, and if you will let Him, He will now begin to complete your nature by making it to be what He meant it to be years ago when you were cradled at the foot of the cross."—*F. B. Meyer.*

JEREMIAH goes down into the lower city, or into the valley between the upper and the lower city, and there his attention is arrested by a potter sitting at his work before a wheel. As the prophet watches a vessel is spoiled in the making under the craftsman's hand; so the process begins afresh and out of the same lump of clay another vessel is molded according to the potter's fancy.

Jeremiah was in school, though he didn't know it. God had sent him down to the pottery, where he might learn his lesson. Poor Jeremiah! His heart was aching and nearly breaking because his attempts to save the people from destruction seemed utterly futile. Here, in the clay-pit, his attention is called to a potter who is busy fashioning a lump of clay into lovely form, when, lo! just as it was being completed, it crumbled to pieces beneath the work man's hand. Some of the fragments fell upon the wheel, and some upon the ground. He thought that the potter would let them go and take another chunk of clay, but instead, he gathered up the broken pieces and began to make them over.

The lesson seems to teach the possibility of recovery from failure by, a second trial, even with the same material. The failure on the part of the potter was not due to poor workmanship, but to poor clay. What is the matter that you have not reached your ideal? Has God failed? No. What is the matter? Poor clay. It will have to be worked over. God has to reshape us a good many times before He can get anything very comely out of the brittle fragments of our lives. He can make use of the clay if it is of any account at all.

The design of the potter is often frustrated by a defect in the clay. It may be only after repeated attempts with the same material that his object is achieved. God's work has always been hindered by human flaws. Even a slight defect may mar a soul, but here is a parable that teaches that it is possible to re-form the heart; that the broken pieces of a shattered life are worth picking up. Disheartened child, take courage! Some of God's best saints had to be made over. Jacob, supplanter, wily bargainer, conniving plotter, when he is made over becomes Israel, prince of God, father of a nation. Saul of Tarsus, unrelenting persecutor, becomes Paul the Apostle, mighty exponent of the Christian faith. Peter, trembling coward, is converted into the fearless preacher. The majority of lives are marred and have to be made over. There is still a chance for every broken life to be re-shaped.

The Divine Potter is constantly working with human clay, but even He can do nothing with material which is not plastic in His hands. Man has furnished Him such poor earth that the vessel is often broken in His hand, but He is patient and will gather up the pieces and try again. He does the work so quietly and unostentatiously that man sometimes feels that he has done it himself. It is said of Herkomer, the great artist, that after he had come to name and fame in London, that he sent for his father, a simple wood-chopper from the Black Forest, and desired that he should spend the rest of his days with him. The old gentleman was fond of molding things out of clay, but as he grew older and his form trembled with the palsy of weakness, he often went upstairs at night disappointed, feeling that his hand was losing its cunning. After the father was safe in bed, the gifted son would go down and make it over into beautiful form, and in the morning the old man would look with pleasure upon what he thought to be his own work. God often has to do that with us. Is your life marred? Give God a chance to make it over.

PROJECTED EFFICIENCY

"I must work the works of Him that sent Me."—*St. John ix, 4.*

"I have never heard anything about the resolutions of the apostles, but a great deal about their acts."—*Horace Mann.*

"I can do all things through Christ which strengtheneth me."
—*Philippians iv, 13.*

"Life was not given for indolent contemplation and study of self, nor for brooding over emotions of piety; actions and actions only determine the worth."—*Fichte.*

"Whatsoever thy hand findeth to do, do it with thy might."
—*Ecclesiastes ix, 10.*

"Be great in act as you have been in thought. Suit the action to the word and the word to the action."—*Shakespeare.*

IN any sense in which the terms may be used, there is a vast difference between efficiency and *projected* efficiency. Efficiency is the state of possessing adequate knowledge or ability for the performance of a duty or function. Projected efficiency is knowledge or ability acting in accordance with a plan previously sketched out and forecasted. The former is subjective, the latter is objective; the one is passive and may use its ability only to hold the fort, the other is active and shows a determination both to hold its own and to storm and take another fort. An automobile stands at the curb quivering with energy and with every fiber of its mechanism trembling with power—that is efficiency. A man steps into the car, pulls a lever, applies the force, turns the guide-wheel, and the huge machine whirls swiftly down the avenue—that is projected efficiency.

We are proceeding on the assumption that the fact of existence implies its necessity; that to be alive and to have the right use of one's faculties is to possess somewhat of talent, and that to possess *any* talent is to be under the obligation of using it. Truly enough, the existence of some men is of greater importance to the world than that of others; but to be an individual is to be God-sent, and that is to have a mission. There is something each one is able to do, and, in consequence of this ability, something that both God and fellow-man have a right to expect him to do. Some minimizer of private soul-worth has said, "If you wish an illustration of your importance in the world, stick your finger in the ocean, and, having with drawn it, look for the hole." But, notwithstanding the seeming truth of the statement, each person has his place to fill, and if he do not fill it he creates an eternal void. It would be a fearful thing to die and leave one's errand unfulfilled.

Each soul has a certain kind of efficiency. He has a vital relationship to his own group. He is able to do a particular thing, and his talent is wrapped in a napkin and hidden in the earth until he has projected his value in some kind of a positive deed. There are too many people in the world who are the mere passive recipients of impressions which, in reality, take no firm hold upon them. They are like weather vanes, which turn to suit the direction of the wind. They cherish no truth strongly; there is no passion in their life.

Goodness in its last analysis is greatness, but goodness in action is the greatest goodness. It is not enough simply to be good—one must be good for something. The man of real value to the world has a program. He is justly conscious of the possession of power and his life is filled with a commanding purpose. He is no figure-head; he is a man in fact. He possesses opinions and a will; he has convictions, the holding of which is dearer to him than life.

The irresolute person thinks, and moralizes, and dreams, and does nothing. The life that reaches the full measure of its possibility must be under the mastery of a regnant, righteous will. The will is the executive of the conscience, and the conscience whose dictates are not enforced is worthless. It is related that the first Lord Shaftesbury, in a conversation with Locke, said that wisdom lay in the heart, not the head, and that it was not want of knowledge, but perverseness of will that filled men's actions with folly and their lives with disorder. Even good will is not enough—one must act in accordance with good will.

The difference between efficiency and projected efficiency is in reality the difference between weakness and strength. When Luther said to Erasmus, "You wish to walk on eggs without crushing them, and on glasses without breaking them," the timorous, hesitating Erasmus replied, "I will not be unfaithful to the cause of Christ, at least, *so far as the age will permit.*" Luther was of a different type. He said in substance: "It is my duty to go to the Diet with this matter, and I will go if I encounter devils as numerous as the tiles on the housetops, and though I should have to go through flames that reach from Worms to Wittenberg and flash up to heaven, and though it rain Duke Georges for nine days together." The first question after a right course of action has presented itself, is not, "What will the people say?" but, "Is it my duty?" Some men of willingness and ability fail through lack of courage. There are a lot of people in the world who are sweet-spirited and passively good, but there is a sin-cursed world to be saved, and it will never be redeemed by retiring righteousness. God wants some spirit-filled fighters who can strike terrific blows and make deep gashes and smite to the death. Sin can not be conquered in a mild way. The world can not be saved by philosophers who quibble and discuss, but by decisive men who act.

THE DIET OF THE SOUL

"Wherefore do you spend money for that which is not bread? and your labor for that which satisfieth not? hearken diligently to Me, and eat ye that which is good, and let your soul delight itself in fatness."
—*Isaiah lv, 2.*

"A fig for your bill-of-fare; show me your bill of company."—*Swift.*

"Labor not for the meat which perisheth, but for that which endureth ... I am the living bread that comes down from heaven; if any man eat of this bread he shall live forever."—*St. John vi, 27, 51.*

"If thou wouldst preserve a strong body, use fasting and walking; if a healthful soul, fasting and praying. Walking exercises the body; praying the soul; fasting cleanses both."—*Quarles.*

WHAT to eat is a matter of serious consideration, especially for those who are weak or ill. Nourishment has a direct relation to health and happiness. One may be rendered unfit for service either by starvation or luxury. The one lowers his vitality and opens the way for disease; the other poisons his system and loads him with weakness, excesses, and abuse. Life depends upon what it assimilates, and is best sustained by a wholesome diet. It is better to enrich its powers by nourishment than to quicken its activity by stimulant. The food one eats becomes literally his blood, his flesh, his life. He gets its strength not by talking about it, looking at it, nor by admiring its nutritive properties; but by feeding upon it. There is the closest possible relation between the body and the things upon which it lives. It is, therefore, of the utmost importance that the dietary be simple and good. It must be neither scanty nor sumptuous, but plain, generous, and substantial. It is of relatively greater importance that one should have a care about the diet of his soul.

Spiritual health is vitally related to the food upon which the soul subsists. One may starve his heart or nourish it according as he allows it to feed on the husks of sin or the finest wheat of God's good harvest. Starved souls are not in need so much of medicine as of wholesome food. The Gospel must not be minimized as a remedy for sin, but it ought to be magnified as a means of nourishing spiritual soundness. It becomes such a means not when we read about Christ, or talk about Him, but only when we feed upon His life and assimilate all that was in it of inspiration and power.

When the prophet said, "Eat ye that which is good," he was speaking to the Hebrew captives in Babylon on the eve of their return to Jerusalem. Babylon was the center of the world's trade. It was during their exile here that the Jews formed their mercantile habits, which, next to their religion or in place of it, have become the genius of their national character. Their toil had borne fruit. They had gathered property and were settled in outward comfort. But, however prosperous, they were unable to satisfy their highest cravings on the things which money could buy in a strange country. Home, to Israel, meant Jerusalem, duty, righteousness, God. Their real hunger and thirst were for Jehovah, and in Him alone could they find the delightsome fatness of their soul. It is ever so. Commercial prosperity and material success have no power to purchase satisfaction for the heart that is not rich toward God. The luxuries of wealth only taunt the hunger of the soul that does not feed on that which is good. Riches is a mockery when the heart has no treasure in heaven. It is a crime to feed the body and starve the soul, but is still worse to compel the soul to feed upon the things which will destroy it.

Christ, using human conditions and attempting to signify His relation to His followers, in metaphor, said, "I am the Door," or, "I am the Vine," or, "I am the Light," or, "I am the Way," or, "I am the Good Shepherd," and then, in recognition of heart-hunger and in full knowledge of what would satisfy it, declared that He was the Bread of Life, and that any soul that would feed on Him should live.

The diet of the soul determines its quality. One's very nature is changed into the similitude of the things on which he feeds. Beasts are rendered ferocious by feeding them on uncooked meat. The food one eats even leaves its impress on his countenance. The contrast between Daniel's fair face and the countenances of his dissipated attendants is explained by the difference between plain food and the sumptuous gluttony of the king's court. The student's face is radiant with intelligence, and one's religious tone may be detected in his visage. It is not necessary to be in the presence of a person long to be able to determine at what table he satisfies his hunger.

There is a deeper hunger than the unholy cravings of the life of sin. The diet of the soul should satisfy the deepest cravings of the heart. The sot, reeking with a life of debauch when he enters the mission and breaks down and sobs and repents, gives expression to a hunger different from the sensual cravings of a life of sin The Bread of Life will satisfy that longing. Truth must be embodied in living form before man can live upon it. Physical life can only be sustained by that which has been alive. Truth in the abstract is hard to assimilate, but when the Word becomes flesh, we can feed upon it. The Bread of Life is not a luxury; it is a necessity. Feed on it by faith.

THE MEDICINES OF THE SOUL

"I went unto the angel and said unto him, Give me the little book. And he said unto me, Take it and eat it up."—*Revelation x, 9.*

"The books we read should be chosen with great care, that they may be as an Egyptian king wrote over his library, 'The Medicines of the Soul.'"

"Did ye never read in the Scriptures?"—*St. Matthew xxi, 42.*

"Some books are to be tasted, others swallowed, and some few to be chewed and digested."—*Bacon.*

"Understandest what thou readest?"—*The Acts viii, 30.*

"The book to read is not the one that thinks for you, but the one which makes you think. No book in the world equals the Bible for that."
—*McCosh.*

THERE is a certain similarity between a drug-store and a library. The one contains vials filled with lotions, irritants, stimulants, narcotics, balms, and poisons, capable of producing specific effects upon man's physical nature; the other contains volumes filled with substances capable of producing analogous effects upon the mind. It would be exceedingly unwise for any one unskilled in the properties and effects of drugs to fill prescriptions and administer doses; his ignorance might bring destruction and death upon himself and others. It may be equally fatal, though the results are not so quickly apparent, to the soul of man if he deals thus indiscriminately with books.

Never has the statement of the wise man, "Of making many books there is no end," been more true than now. America, England, and France together publish more than twenty-five thousand volumes annually. Only a small percentage at best of this enormous output can ever exert any potent influence on life or thought. The danger lies in the fact that so many people have not the power to discriminate between the valueless and low-grade fiction, and that wholesome literature that is a tonic to mind and heart alike. Some of the poorest trash is often bound in most attractive style. When Carlyle said, "The true university is a collection of books," he had in mind only books worth reading. If he were here today he would say, "Choose your books and read a few good ones rather than many poor ones." We are sometimes ashamed to admit that we are not acquainted with some new and much-discussed novel, when the truth of the matter is that it might be a waste of time and energy even to read it. It is always safe, when a new book comes out, to read an old one that has stood the test of time. The books that really furnish food for life will live beyond a year. Good books, like good hearts, improve with age. The trashy pabulum of sensational literature is liable to produce mental indigestion. Read the best first, whether old or new; if you have time, read the rest, is safe advice.

If books are "The Medicines of the Soul," one should choose his author with the same care as he would select his physician. We do not want a doctor to prescribe for our bodily ailments, or even to hand us an advertisement of his concoctions, if he do not know poison from soothing syrup. Why should we permit any man to hand us or sell us an advertisement of his mind if he know no distinction between moral cleanliness and immoral filth? In the realm of written thought the world is full of good things and cheap, but the wise man will select.

We take medicine to assist nature in making our bodies sound; we should read such books as help our minds to grow both strong and well. Medicine is doing most for the body when it is enriching the blood, building up the constitution and strengthening its functional activity. Books with truly medicinal properties enrich the soul-life and contribute to its largest and completest development. The books that really nourish us are those which bring us self-revelation. The physician who can properly diagnose a case can find the seat of the trouble; it is easy then to prescribe a cure if any remedy is known. If you would have your moral ill revealed, read the Bible. You may find the cure there, too. There is but one book; there is but one physician; there is but one remedy. There are many good books, but all the good of all the books is found in God's good Book. Wherever you find good you find God, and whenever you feed your soul on good you contribute to its welfare.

A LARGE PLACE

"He brought me forth into a large place." —*The Psalms xviii, 19.*

"There are two freedoms; the false, where man is free to do what he likes; the true, where man is free to do what he ought."—*Kingsley.*

"To an honest mind the best prerequisites of a place are the advantages it gives a man of doing good."—*Addison.*

"Reflect upon your present blessings, of which every man has many; not on your past misfortunes, of which all men have some."—*Dickens.*

"It is not the place that maketh the person, but the person that maketh the place honorable."—*Cicero.*

THE eighteenth Psalm is justly considered one of the most magnificent odes that David ever wrote. It is a song of deliverance. He sang it in the last years of his prosperity, when all the surrounding nations were bowing in homage and presenting to him their tribute. The title of the poem states that the words were spoken by David in the day that the Lord delivered him from the hand of all his enemies, and from the hand of Saul. It is an outburst of thanksgiving from the heart for God's manifold and marvelous blessings, and has its historical setting in the relationship of the author with the jealous king.

He has been persecuted sorely, compelled to live in forest and cave like a hunted fox, and now that he feels that he has been delivered from Saul and all the rest of his enemies, it is little wonder that he feels that he has come out into a large place.

We are inclined to belittle our spheres of usefulness and to feel that our place in the world is small and obscure and that our influence is narrow and circumscribed. Our fields are really larger than we think, even though at times they seem to be contracted by bondage and oppression. At all events, the delights of freedom are accentuated by the knowledge of the servitude from which we have been delivered, and he who has been forced into a small place enjoys the expanse of a large one. The freed slave has a right to sing of liberty and to exult in the praise of his deliverer. There is a large place for every soul. Only the one who trusts in God can expect Almighty deliverance. When the Romans under Marcus Aurelius, in an expedition against the Gauls, found themselves hungry and tormented with thirst and facing inevitable defeat because they were surrounded by precipitous mountains occupied by their barbarian foe, the commander of the Praetorian guards informed the emperor that the Militine legions were Christians and believed in the efficacy of prayer. Aurelius thereupon commanded them to conjure their God. Hardly had they arisen from their knees when, according to the pagan historian, a terrific storm of hail and lightning, as if it were fire and water from the clouds, frightened and drove the Quadi from their intrenchments to seek relief among the Romans, where only a gentle and refreshing rain was falling. Call it coincidence or what you will, there are many facts in history, ancient and modern, which seem to justify the belief that the soul that trusts in God can command the infinite resources of Almightiness.

One of the evident and admirable traits of the author of this poem is that he *remembers* his deliverance from the deep waters. Man is so prone to forget the benefits of God. The English proverb puts it, "The river past and God forgotten," while the Italian form sounds sadder still, "The trial passed, the saint mocked." Man's memory seems to fade in proportion as the distance between himself and the past experience increases. Mandrabulus, the Samian, under the auspices and direction of Juno, discovered a gold mine. In his instant gratitude he vowed to her a golden ram, which he presently exchanged in intention to a silver one, and again this for a very small brass one, and this for nothing at all.

A man's religion is his life, and can not be disassociated from his thought and work. His daily deeds are the measure of what he has a right to expect from God. God deals with men as men deal with one another. David had a right to regard his deliverance as a reward of his righteous dealings with Saul. We get back our mete as we measure. We have a right to expect forgiveness only as we forgive. Pope feels this when he prays:

> "Teach me to feel another's woe;
> To hide the fault I see;
> The mercy I to other's show,
> That mercy Show to me."

When God frees a man from the enemies of his soul, He enlarges his possibilities. The new man in Christ Jesus is a man of larger usefulness. But there is a very real sense in which one must work out his own salvation. The only large place a man will ever fill will be the one that he has made for himself. It is a mercy to man that he is asked to make his own promotion. If it were not so, he might experience the ridiculous situation of being a little man in a big place—a terrible calamity. Right is stronger than might, and "Truth crushed to earth will rise again," and when it does it will be in a larger place. No one can be at his best when driven by the enemy of his soul into the barren fastnesses of life, where he must skulk and hide in caves and darkness, afraid to sally forth. But with God's deliverance there comes freedom—the freedom of a larger place.

A DIVIDED HEART

"Their heart is divided."—*Hosea x, 2.*

"Either take Christ into your lives, or cast Him out of your lips. Either be what thou seemest, or else be what thou art."—*Dyer.*

"In religion, not to do as thou sayest is to unsay thy religion in thy deeds and to undo thyself by doing."—*Vanning.*

"No man can serve two masters; for either he will hate the one and love the other; or else he will hold to the one and despise the other."
—*St. Matthew vii, 24.*

"There is no class of men so difficult to be managed in a state as those whose intentions are honest but whose consciences are bewitched."
—*Napoleon.*

HOSEA got his conception of the consequences of a divided heart in one of the saddest experiences that can fall to the lot of human life. In a day of unspeakable sorrow he awoke to the fact that his home was wrecked; that the wife of his youth, the companion of his heart's love, the mother of his boy, had proven false to her marriage vows. Immeasurable abyss of grief! What anguish of soul when he was forced to name the second-born "Unpitied," and the third, "Not Mine!" O, heart-rending pathos—a child made orphan by a mother's sin!

Hosea looked about him and saw that his experience was not unique; that other homes were broken by divided hearts. In this wreck-age and debris of sin he caught a vision of the apostate child of God. In the hurt of his own heart, in his longing for the return of his prodigal wife, he came to an appreciation of the wounded patience of an outraged God whose children had broken their covenant and wronged His love. He shows that his wife had sinned through ignorance, and in the vain belief that her corn and wine and oil and increased gold and silver were gifts of paramours. She did not know that it was he, her true love, who had given her bread and water and wool and flax. In his personal experience, the prophet has come upon the Lord's view-point when he declares, "My people are destroyed through lack of knowledge." God is grieved because Israel has forsaken His love. They are falling from bad to worse, and their trouble is subjective—"Their heart is divided."

It is impossible to build a home on divided sentiments; it is equally impossible for a heart to be at peace and have a divided aim. Unity is absolutely necessary to strength. A divided heart is a weak heart—it will break itself and others. It is both unstable and unhappy. The right way is the way of the true heart; it is not always easy, but when one keeps in it he feels satisfied. It is impossible for one with even a spark of conscience to do wrong and feel right. The strong heart is devoted to a single Lord.

The majority of people who acknowledge no definite relationship to the Kingdom of God are not atheists nor infidels, but simply persons without settled convictions. So many persons are unwilling to take a stand on a principle of known right because of fear, love of pleasure or gain, or for the sake of policy. These are not men—they are only so many figures for sale on the open market! At the mercy of the trade-winds of public opinion and with no fixed course, they point at irregular intervals at every star in the social universe; with no courage to decide, they halt between two opinions until the best part of life is frittered away. Most people know better than they do. The weakness of the Church has ever been that so many of its members have a theory of religion for Sunday and another for working hours; one code of ethics for the sanctuary and another for the board of trade. It is absolutely outside the range of possibility to be part in one kingdom and part in another. God will either rule the heart or vacate.

A house built on divided interests can not stand, and a soul can not serve both God and mammon. Stability of character can only rest on a fixed center of right. A righteous man is not charged with some sort of ethereal luminosity that makes his face glow with a ghostly sheen; he is simply a man of unflinching integrity and uncompromising honor, with a single aim, based on a sane conception of right, and a stanch purpose unalterably fixed and constant as Polaris. This high-grade life can not be obtained without much prayer and effort. I call you to the undivided service of a true and honest heart. To love the Lord with all one's soul and mind and might is the surest road to ultimate and abundant success in life. A true Christian is only a man at his best.

THE MAN OF GOD

"That the man of God may be complete, thoroughly furnished."
—*2 Timothy iii, 17.*

"Let each man think himself an act of God; his mind a thought, his life a breath of God."—*Bailey.*

"The older I grow—and now I stand on the brink of eternity—the more comes back to me that sentence in the Catechism, which I learned when a child, and the fuller and deeper its meaning becomes, 'What is the chief end of man? To glorify God and enjoy Him forever.'"—*Carlyle.*

"God divided man into men, that they might help each other." —*Seneca.*

"They that deny a God, destroy man's nobility, for man is akin to the beasts by his body, and if he is not akin to God by his spirit he is an ignoble creature."—*Bacon.*

"Two men please God—who serves Him with all his heart because he knows Him; who seeks Him with all his heart because he knows Him not."—*Panin.*

THE expression, "Man of God," is usually construed in a general way and applied to mankind of either sex. For the sake of directing special attention to the masculine division of the human race, permit me to use it in the literal sense and to raise the question of the relation of a *man* to the Kingdom of God.

The average congregation in the modern Church has a greater percentage of ladies than gentlemen. Who can produce the reason? It has not always been so. The first persons attracted by the teachings of Jesus were men. The great champions of the faith all through the ages have, for the most part, been men. There must be some reason for the fact that men apparently are less interested in the Church and the outward forms of religion than formerly. Has Christianity lost its virile strength, or have men so lapsed into a condition of stupid lethargy that their hearts no longer respond to the call of Truth? It is sometimes charged that the presentation of the Gospel is weak and effeminate: but such accusations are usually made by those who seldom or never go to

Church. It is more likely to be true that whenever men do not delight in the services of the sanctuary it is because they have lost their taste for spiritual things. It is not fair to judge a man's virtue by his religiousness; there is a vast difference between that and religion; but it is just to assume that he who has any hunger for righteousness will embrace every opportunity to feed upon the things which satisfy it. The Temple stands for God's visible presence in the world, and myriads of souls have found meat in its ministrations. He who has no relish for the House of Prayer must have a depraved appetite.

Who, then, is the man of God? Is he a preacher? Yes, a preacher ought to be a man of God. But, is he necessarily a person who devotes his whole time to things openly and formally religious? No! In the very most real sense, any virtuous business man is a man of God. Each man who has a sense of the dignity of life realizes that he is here on business for his King. He has no business that is not God's business, and if he be dishonorable by the measurement of a hair's breadth, he is untrue to the divine stamp of manhood. He who is unswervingly conscientious, undeviatingly consistent, and constantly reliable is a man of God.

If a man be not God's man, whose man is he? No sane man is irresponsible. Every man of sound mind is working in the interest of somewhat and ought to be conscious of the great privilege, as well as the great responsibility, of possessing power to control the issues of his life. Man is so constituted that he feels the sense of being possessed—he is fully aware that he serves the master whom he obeys. The question is, therefore, pertinent: If a man be not a man of God, what kind of a man is he?

The man of God is simply the highest type of thoroughly furnished manhood—a person who uses all his powers and abuses none. He realizes his stewardship and gives an accurate account of himself. He tries to live at the top of his condition, physically, mentally, morally. He is religious because he knows that one can not disregard his relation to God and ever be complete. He finds his heart going out after something beyond and above himself. He finds the object that satisfies his cravings and is naturally worshipful. He acknowledges the image in which he has been created and seeks to bring no dishonor upon his heritage. He fears God and loves Him because he believes that life is no farce, religion no fable, and that godliness is profitable in this world and the next. A man is a poor man who is not a man of God.

WORK AND WORSHIP

"Thou shalt worship the Lord thy God, and Him only shalt thou serve."—*St. Luke iv, 8.*

"Not alone to know, but to act according to thy knowledge, is thy destination, proclaims the voice of thy inmost soul. Not for indolent contemplation and study of thyself, nor for brooding over emotions of piety—no, for action was existence given thee; thy actions and thy actions alone determine thy worth."—*Fichte.*

"Lord, who shall abide in Thy tabernacle? . . . He that *walketh* uprightly and *worketh* righteousness."—*Psalm xv, 1, 2.*

"We should worship as though the Deity were present. If my mind is not engaged in my worship, it is as though I worshiped not."
—*Confucius.*

"Faith, if it hath not works is dead."—*St. James ii, 17.*

CARLYLE once said, "What greater calamity can fall upon a nation than the loss of worship?" He also said, "The latest gospel in the world is, Know thy work and do it." Work and worship go hand in hand. Spirituality depends as much upon work as work upon spirituality. To disregard worship is to be an in grate; to fail to do one's work is to thwart the plans of God. Failing to understand the interrelation of these terms, men go to one of two extremes— they separate themselves from the world of work to live a life of prayer; or, they rely upon their deeds alone to make good their lack of faith. The world has been slow to learn that one's deeds can not be divorced from his devotions. Though worship is a condition of man's soul, an instinct of his life, it took him a long time to grasp the thought, "God is a spirit, and they that worship Him must worship Him in spirit and in truth;" and seemingly, he only partially appreciates yet the fact that his life interprets his prayers.

In his primitive state man worshiped, but he had to have something visible on which to fasten his eyes. He found this object in nature—as the sun, a river, a mountain, a lake—or he constructed an image with his own hands out of wood, or metal, or stone. As he grew in wisdom and capacity of understanding he began to look within, and, by a divinely appointed introspection, saw the true altar, the true sanctuary, the true center of acceptable worship. It was only after his piety began to feed itself on the almightiness of God that he came to perceive that "God is a spirit." Ancient Judaism kept up a magnificent tragedy of symbolism, but modern Christianity must represent an infinitely more magnificent tragedy of reality. When the heart is right, conduct will be right, and worship becomes the adoring reverence of the human spirit for the divine, seeking outward expression. God cares not for priestly pomp—He wants personal purity.

> "He asks no taper lights on high, surrounding
>   The priestly altar and the saintly grave;
> No dolorous chant nor organ music sounding,
>   Nor incense clouding up the twilight nave.
>
> For he whom Jesus loved has truly spoken
>   The holier worship which He deigns to bless
> Restores the lost, and binds the spirit-broken,
>   And feeds the widow and the fatherless."

Work is the generic term for any continuous application of energy toward an end. Worship is the feeling or the act of religious homage toward deity. Worship expresses an attitude, work an activity; worship adores, work achieves; worship prays, work performs; worship is exaltation, work is exertion; worship does homage to deity, work does honor to duty. While work and worship seem so opposite in certain characteristics, they are at the same time so inseparably united as almost to be identical. True worship can never be an externality nor a thing apart from the tasks of life; it is not the reading of rites nor the mumbling of masses—it is the overflow of a spirit-filled life; it is the aroma of good works. He who works rightly worships rightly.

No man can worship who does not work. He who thinks that he can come to the sanctuary on Sunday and in a few spasms of prayer straighten out a week of crooked work, is deceived. God looks upon work well done as the best homage of a true heart. Prayers that do not harmonize with practice have no wings; they simply flutter and fall; they are dead, worthless things. Worship that pleases God is a spontaneity; it bubbles up out of life's daily task; it can not be forced; it can not be put on; it must spring from the depths. Study a man's life if you want to know the value of his prayers. The quality of his worship is determined by the standard of his work. There can be no symphony of worship without symmetry of work. Life must be a song of work and worship.

REMEMBERING ONE'S FAULTS

"I do remember my faults this day."—*Genesis xli, 9*.

"The greatest of faults is to be conscious of none."—*Carlyle*.

"Ten thousand of the greatest faults in our neighbors are of less consequence to us than one of the smallest in our-selves."—*Whately*.

"Cleanse thou me from hidden faults."—*Psalm xix, 12*.

"No one sees the wallet on his own back, though every one carries two packs; one before, stuffed with the faults of his neighbors; the other behind, filled with his own."—*Old Proverb*.

"In their mouth was found no guile; for they are without fault before the throne of God."—*Revelation xiv, 5*.

"We should correct our own faults by seeing how un-comely they appear in others."—*Beaumont*.

A FAULT is defined as a slight offense; a neglect of duty or propriety, resulting from inattention or lack of prudence rather than from design to injure or offend; Whatever impairs excellence; a blemish; a defect.

A thing may be approximately perfect and still have faults. Faults represent the difference between the work of an amateur and that of a master. They are the defects which a critic's eye would notice. They may be due to inability or inexperience; to carelessness or crudity. The difference between work fairly well done and work done as well as it can be, may not seem great: but it is the difference between the faulty and the faultless; the difference between the product of Michael Angelo and that of the ordinary sculptor; between the handiwork of Raphael and that of the painter of common note; between the designs of Von Rile and those of the average architect of splendid halls. The significance of this difference is in the question of how much the defect damages and of how much more a faultless thing is worth. One man takes a certain number of paints, canvas of a certain shape and size, brushes of a certain variety, and paints a picture which he sells for twenty-five dollars;

another man takes the same kind of paints, the same shape and size of canvas, and the very same brushes, and paints a picture which he sells for twenty-five thousand dollars—the difference between these sums is the price of a fault so small that the untrained eye could scarcely see it at all. The difference between the faulty and the faultless is a matter of no little importance.

With reference to character, persons unwilling to admit that they have sinned are very ready to acknowledge that they have faults. It is quite common to look upon a fault as something less than a sin. In fact, there are those who seem to be rather proud of their eccentricities and idiosyncrasies, as if they were noteworthy marks of private personality. Faults of the heart can not, however, be dismissed with no concern. In calling to mind the things which subtract from perfection, discount our influence and our life, which blemish our characters, and which impair the completeness of our work, we must consider by how much the value of our being is lessened by our faults and how defective our lives may be, and still be regarded by an all-wise and impartial Judge as sufficiently meritorious to be entitled to the reward of the righteous. In other words, how much less than perfect can we be and still be received, in the end, as if we were perfect?

One's faults are the weak places at which his character is liable to break. A heart like a chain is really no stronger than its weakest point. Defects always discount; a blemished beast or a damaged thing will not bring full price. The flaw may be insignificant, but it is always noted and a price is set upon it. A soul may be sound in ninety-nine items in a hundred, and yet the one may work the destruction of the many. The virtue of a life that is truly honest at the core may run out through the leak of a very small defect. Good men often pay dreadful penalties for a single break in honor.

It is a good thing for one to examine himself and to test his heart for flaws, weak places, and defects. It is easy to see the faults of others, but not so easy to see our own, because we will not try. There are parts of our lives, past and present, which we do not like to think about, but from which we may learn useful les sons. A mere incident or conjunction of circumstances may bring them to our mind. There is no value in remembering our faults if we only look at our actions to try to make them seem as white as possible; we must be severe with ourselves if our investigation amount to anything worth while.

When one remembers his faults he realizes how hard it is for God to establish His kingdom in the face of such obstacles. The question of faults is a serious one, for the heart must be without them, excepting the infirmities which it can not control, before it is fit for heaven. We pray, "Thy kingdom come," and our faults belie our prayers. Man must attempt to rectify his own faults before he can command the help of God. Listen! Your so-called shortcomings are not trivialities. Minus completeness means weighed and found wanting. It is no slight thing to bring a blemished victim to the altar. Help me, Lord, to clear myself of hidden faults!

IMMORTALITY

"If a man die shall he live again?"—*Job xiv. 14*.

"I am fully convinced that the soul is indestructible, and that its activity will continue through eternity. It is like the sun, which, to our eyes, seems to set in night, but it has in reality only gone to diffuse its light elsewhere."—*Goethe*.

"Not all the subtilities of metaphysics can make me doubt a moment of the immortality of the soul, and of a beneficient providence. I feel it, I believe it, I hope it, and I will defend it to my last breath."—*Rousseau*.

"This mortal must put on immortality."—*1 Corinthians xv, 53*.

GRANT that the universe is the product of a supreme, originating intelligence, and Job's query must be answered in the affirmative. Given God, with the attributes of righteous Deity, and belief in the immortality of the soul is a necessity. Eternal life is not simply a doctrine; it is an essential part of the divine nature. The creation of man "in the image of God" marks him a minor divinity and makes him immortal. We might rest the matter here—it is enough. By divine fiat man bears the likeness of God. There is no more reason why we should assay to prove the natural man immortal than that we should undertake to demonstrate that the same man is rational.

Immortality is not merely a dogma of the Church, and it does not rest solely on the teaching of the Christian Scriptures. It is firmly grounded in the human constitution and inextricably interwoven with the innermost consciousness of being. It is naturally a part of religion. The belief in life after death has existed where the Christian Church and the Bible have never been known or accepted. Plato believed in a future state, and Socrates taught the doctrine of the immortal life. Mankind universally and in all ages have had some idea of existence beyond the grave in some heaven, Elysian field, or happy land. Only blighting rationalism and benumbing satiety can render one indifferent to the destiny of his soul. Pitiful and tragic beyond the power of words is the weakening faith in a divine universe ordered with an ethical purpose, which pretends to argue that man is not free from the law that affects all the lower forms of life. "Woe to the age steeped in luxury and wallowing in wealth, which, having lost its finer enthusiasms and forward-reachings of the soul, settles down to a glorification of its own power and throws to the winds its inheritance of ennobling and inspiring religious beliefs." Its doom is as certain as that of ancient Rome, which tottered and reeled and staggered and fell down through sensuality to destruction.

It is difficult for a soul to rid itself of the feeling and to school itself out of the belief that there is a beyond, something farther on and farther up than the life it now is living. Its very sense of present incompleteness indicates that it has limits which can not be set in calculable spaces; that it is a spark of the Infinite. It is easy to agree with Aristotle that the something within us that feels, thinks, desires, and animates, is celestial, divine, and consequently imperishable. We do not wonder that Cicero, contemplating the marvelous possibilities of the human soul, declared: "When I consider the wonderful activity of the mind, so great a memory of what is past, and such a capacity for penetrating into the future; when I behold such a number of arts and sciences, and such a multitude of discoveries thence arising, I believe and am firmly persuaded that a nature that contains so many things within itself can not but be immortal."

Man's immortality is suggested by his do minion. He is ruler by divine right over earth and sky and sea. His genius knows no bounds. He handles powers which he little understands. He adapts, combines, and within certain limitations creates. He subdues kingdoms and works righteousness and reigns in the realm of virtue. No such power is delegated to the creatures of a day. God loves man because man is like Him, and God's present care for man is presumptive proof of immortality. It is unthinkable that the Lord would order man's steps, number the hairs of his head, pity him with a father's care, make him an angel's charge, bear him up with wings as of eagles, and then say at the end of the earthly career, "Thy end is nothingness and thy fate annihilation." To deny immortality makes God irrational. The world itself is not wasteful, but salvatory. In the midst of apparent decay everything is climbing up and marching on. Man builds his houses to outlast a lifetime, and hands on his treasure from generation to generation. God would not endow a man with the accumulated treasures of a thousand years only to dissolve him in death and blast him in extinction.

Man's immortality is implied in the untimely events that mark the limits of his unfinished work. Think you when a brilliant scholar is obliged to lay down his pen on the page of a half-written volume that his work is done! Nay, the curtain has only dropped between us and him; it can not be that he is not working still. Man dies with his faculties undeveloped. His reason, imagination, conscience, love, need a second Summer for bloom and fruitage. This is what Victor Hugo meant when on his death-bed he said: "For half a century I have been writing my thoughts in prose, verse, history, philosophy, drama, romance, tradition, satire, ode, and song. I have tried all, but I feel that I have not said the thousandth part of what is in me. When I go down to the grave I can say that I have finished my day's work, but I can not say that I have finished my life. The nearer I approach death the clearer I hear around me the immortal symphonies of the world about me. My work is only beginning. My thirst for the Infinite proves infinity." There seems to be an instinct of immortality in man which grows into an experience as the soul draws near the portals of the spirit-world. Lord Byron testified that he felt his immortality oversweep his pains, his time, his fears, and peal like the eternal thunders of the deep into his ears the truth—Thou livest forever. The very fact that man has a desire for immortality proves his capacity for it. The heart craves eternal life. Life is discontented with time and is restless in the possession of treasure. It thirsts. It hungers. It is dissatisfied with sense, earth, space. It craves immortality. Emerson says, "Our dissatisfaction with any other solution is the blazing evidence of immortality."

Man's immortality is established in the resurrection of Christ. If the resurrection is a fact, then life after death is a certainty. The evidence of the resurrection is trustworthy and conclusive. Paul states that the risen Lord was seen by Cephas, the twelve, by five hundred brethren at once (the majority of them being alive at the time he made the statement and could have denied the truth of it had they chosen), by James, by all the apostles, and last of all by himself. His citations ought to be strong enough to establish the fact in any reasonable mind. If Jesus lived after what men call death, then I shall live. If this be true, then the responsibility is on me to live not only for time, but also for eternity. I must remember that the hereafter is the after here; life beyond the grave is only a continuation of the present journey without the "impedimenta." The hereafter is separated from the here only by a narrow vale of darkening mists. O Easter joy! break through the blackness. O clouds! roll back and let me see what is beyond. O Easter faith! let me catch a glimpse of daybreak when the shadows flee away.

THE HEART OF CHRISTMAS

"The Babe lying in a manger."—*St. Luke ii, 16.*

"All history is incomprehensible without Christ."—*Renan.*

"A little child shall lead them."—*Isaiah xi, 6.*

"As little as humanity will ever be without religion, as little will it be without Christ."—*Strauss.*

"Glory to God in the highest, and on earth peace, goodwill toward men."—*St. Luke ii, 14.*

IN an evening paper on the Saturday before Christmas I read a statement to the effect that certain entertainments had been given in the public schools of a certain city the day before. The article was headed "Christmas Exercises," with the following descriptive sub-line, "Entertainments given at the Schools in Honor of Yuletide." The writer had inadvertently borne testimony to the mixing of ideas in our modern Christmas celebrations.

I saw a father buying a Christmas tree, and a woman a wreath of holly, and a young girl a sprig of mistletoe, and I heard a lady say how many presents she had tied up. I read that Santa Claus would entertain in a store-window, that a great chorus was to sing "The Coming of the King," that half a hundred prophets would preach on Christmas, and as many Churches would treat the children to nuts and candy and books. A lot of different ideas, surely! We are told that the ancients celebrated "the return of the sun," when the days began to lengthen after the winter solstice; that the Romans reveled in a feast they called "The Saturnalia," at the same time of the year; that "Yule" was in celebration of the god Thor; that mistletoe was an emblem of the British Druids; that the Christmas tree is a native of Germany; Santa Claus or Saint Nicholas of Holland, and that the plum-pudding is a creation of the English. In the presence of this conglomerate aggregation of conflicting ideas one may well ask, What does Christmas mean? It seems to mean buying and selling, giving and feasting; holly and mistletoe, tinsel and evergreen; singing and

Santa Claus, masses and yuletide; toys and teddy bears, and *exchanging* of presents. But deeper than all the accretions of ages is the true heart of Christmas—the Babe in a manger.

With the emphasis placed on gnomes and sprites and the mixing of pagan ideas with the advent of the King, the world is in danger of forgetting that the heart of Christmas is Christ, and not Santa Claus. Parents may find enough of the miraculous in the story of the birth and life of Jesus to satisfy the imagination of any child without resorting to heathen mythology. The sentiments surrounding the life of the Savior are refined and religious, while those in connection with Santa Claus are crude and superstitious.

Christmas has no meaning without the manger-Babe. You may have a Saturnalia or Yule or Bacchanalian revel, but you can not have Christmas and leave Christ out. It is the birth day anniversary of the infant Lord, and its heart is a child, and not a "teddy bear." A child's playthings should suggest beauty rather than beastliness. The perfection of human nature must always lie in its likeness to childhood.

Christmas-giving is suggested by the fact that God gave His Son to the world to be its Savior. We are to imitate Him and give. The very heart of Christmas is a gift. Too much of the passing about of presents has no love in it. There is a difference between a *gift* and an *exchange*. One may give many gifts, but he never truly keeps Christmas until he is willing to receive from God the gift of peace and give himself to a worthy life. Every gift must be a symbol of the "Unspeakable Gift." Christmas is in honor of the infant Christ. It is not Yuletide: it is Christide. He who would know the heart of Christmas must know the heart of childhood. God's gift to thee is life eternal; thine to Him is service.

GAINS AND LOSSES

"There is a time to get and a time to lose."—*Ecclesiastes iii, 6.*

"Sometimes the best gain is to lose."—*Herbert.*

"In the day of prosperity be joyful, but in the day of adversity consider."—*Ecclesiastes vii, 14.*

"Evil events come from evil causes; and what we suffer, springs generally from what we have done."—*Aristophanes.*

"What is a man profited, if he shall gain the whole world, and lose his own soul?"—*St. Matthew xvi 26.*

> "Tho' the path be rough and thorny
> Bravely bearing up the cross,
> We shall find as on we journey,
> All is gain and nothing loss."

ELIHU, in the drama of Job, about to reprove his aged friends, says, "Days should speak." Days do speak. You may burn the calendar of the old year and hang up a fancy new one in its place; but in the revolving series of days and weeks gone by there are some seasons so marked that they continue to speak and their voices refuse to be stilled. The old year, "being dead, yet speaketh." It speaks of gains and losses, of crowns and crosses. It is vocal with strains which run the gamut of the soul's emotions. It has notes of joy and measures of sorrow, tones of lamentation and scores of rejoicing. Listen! The dying year is speaking.

When we were children we all had an unquestioned belief in the possibility of literally "turning over a new leaf." On the last evening of the year we retired with a feeling that the old was finished, its record closed, and that on the morrow a new year would arrive holding in its hand the most unsullied joy and pleasure. The old self seemed to die with the old year; but alas! it was only seeming. The same old self stands upon the threshold of the new and enters its portals amid the reverberating echoes of the days already numbered.

The days of the past are saying different things to different souls, but to all their voice is speaking. The record is written; the book is closed; but I am not done with the record nor the book. How do I know? The days have told me so. Before we close the book it is, therefore, fitting that we should turn the leaves and look again at the record. Our attitude toward past failure and success will largely determine the meaning of the new year to us.

The wise man in a very pessimistic passage utters the fatalistic statement, "There is a time to get and a time to lose." We may not agree with his philosophy, but we shall surely admit the fact that each life has both times of gain and times of loss. Days of gain are days of rejoicing. The world shouts its acclamations for the Victor whose hands are full of gains. Days of loss are days with sleepless nights. The stem law of the survival of the fittest makes no place for the vanquished loser. Each experience has its own lesson for the soul that wills to learn it. Unbroken prosperity has a tendency to make one selfish in his rejoicing. The measure of man's value is found in his conduct in the day of loss.

There is really only one gain and only one loss. To have laid up a little treasure in heaven is really the only gain; to have fallen below the requisites for citizenship in the Kingdom is really the only loss. You have gained if you have profited by your experiences, whether of prosperity or adversity. You have lost if you have sacrificed your honor, your integrity, or your virtue. You have gained even if you failed while doing your level best. You have lost even though you won by chicanery and fraud. You have gained if all you did was to stand unflinchingly for the right. You have lost if you sacrificed principle to be with the crowd. What have been your gains or losses? Are you climbing higher or slipping back? He who loses heaven loses all, though he gain the world besides.

www.ingramcontent.com/pod-product-compliance
Lightning Source LLC
Chambersburg PA
CBHW020426010526
44118CB00010B/439